ONTARIO GHOST STORIES

BARBARA SMITH

LONE PINE

The Publisher: Lone Pine Publishing

10145-81 Avenue	202A 1110 Seymour Street	1901 Raymond Ave., SW, Suite C
Edmonton, AB T6E 1W9	Vancouver, BC V6B 3N3	Renton, WA 98055
Canada	Canada	USA

Lone Pine Publishing website: http://www.lonepinepublishing.com

Canadian Cataloguing in Publication Data
Smith, Barbara, 1947-
  Ontario ghost stories

  Includes bibliographical references.
  ISBN 1-55105-203-2

  1. Ghosts—Ontario. 2. Legends—Ontario. I. Title.
GR580.S648 1998   133.1'09713   C98-910892-9

Senior Editor: Nancy Foulds
Editorial: Nancy Foulds, Volker Bodegom, Erin McCloskey
Production Manager: David Dodge
Layout and Production: Volker Bodegom
Book Design and Cover Design: Michelle Bynoe
Printing: Webcom Limited, Toronto, Ontario, Canada
Photographs Courtesy of: Candy Alexander (pp. 14, 30); Bob Murdoch (pp. 17, 27); Thousand Islands Playhouse (pp. 49, 191); Grand Theatre, London, Ontario (pp. 68, 77); Elgin and Winter Garden Theatres (p. 73); Royal Alexandra Theatre (p. 83); Town of Whitby Archives (pp. 86, 201); Chiefswood Museum (pp. 105, 117); Robert Salts (p. 109); Wallaceburg and District Museum (p. 135); Hockey Hall of Fame (pp. 155, 165); Kiwanis Collection (p. 172); National Archives of Canada (p. 177); Heritage Toronto (pp. 187, 199, 209); Keg Mansion (p. 205).

The publisher gratefully acknowledges the support of the Department of Canadian Heritage.

Dedication

This book is dedicated, with love, to my favourite Ontario residents: my sister, Joan Arnott, and my brother, Barry Hunter.

For my grandsons and their peers—who will need forests as much as books—arrangements have been made to plant trees to compensate for those used in publishing this volume.

Contents

Acknowledgements

Many people have contributed to this volume. While compiling and writing the book, I have counted on friends and relatives to keep my project in mind as they went about their daily routines. Their assistance has been deeply appreciated, but is not surprising, as these are people I count on for support in all realms of my life. However, the amount of effort that total strangers have graciously volunteered has been utterly amazing and heartwarming to me. I extend a warm thank you to all the people who've shared their intriguing stories with me.

Others have supplied me with important leads or details. I would like to extend a public thank you to these people: Randy Alldread, publicist of Mirvish Productions in Toronto; author Frank Anderson of Saskatoon; my sister, Joan Arnott, of North York; Eleanor Burgess of Ottawa; Ted and Suzanne Currie of Gravenhurst; Alice d'Anjou, freelance film producer in Ottawa; Sandra Bradt of the City of Windsor Tourist Bureau; Ottawa film producer Shannon Fisher; my nephew, Hugh Francisci, of Mississauga; editor Dawn Hunter of Mark My Words in Toronto; my friend, Gloria Hurst, of Mississauga; film producer Michael Jorgensen of First Light Productions; Mix 96 creative director Marty Kreil; librarian Mary Jane Lamb of the St. Lawrence Islands National Park Library; Arnie Lappin of the Elgin and Winter Garden Theatres; Lynn Lefebvre of the Georgina Public Library; publicist Kathryn MacKay of Thousand Islands Playhouse in Gananoque; Bernice Mandryk of Gravenhurst; Kelly Masse of the Hockey Hall of Fame; Bob Murdoch of Severn Bridge; Eileen Nighswander of the Wallaceburg and District Museum; Ginette Peters of the Ontario

Workers Arts and Heritage Centre; Denis Robitaille of the National Library of Canada; author Dr. Barrie Robinson of Edmonton; curator David St. Onge of Canada Corrections Museum in Kingston; Rob Wellan and Sheila Johnston of the Grand Theatre in London; Brian Winter, archivist with the Town of Whitby; Niagara-area historian Sherman Zavitz; and the staff of Edmonton Public Libraries, especially the Inter-library Loan Department.

There are two people whose assistance went well beyond any expectation I could ever have had. The first was paranormal researcher Ritchie Benedict of Calgary, who acted as my unofficial research assistant. The leads from archived newspapers that he sent to me were always accompanied by long, cheery letters. In this day of reasonably priced long-distance telephone calls, letter writing has become almost a lost art. For that reason alone, I'm fortunate to have Ritchie Benedict in my life, but it is his amazing research skill that I most appreciate. Once again, Ritchie, my sincere thanks for your generous contributions to my projects.

In the earliest research stages of this book, I wrote letters to the editors of weekly Ontario newspapers and, as a result, received many original ghost stories. The letter to a Chatham-area paper elicited even more—an offer of research assistance from a geotechnical engineer. Via e-mail, Steve Bartlett and I soon became friends. Thanks to Steve, this book contains many intriguing stories and I have gained an added perception of parts of the world around me—including ghosts.

I would also like to thank the management and staff at Lone Pine Publishing for their consistently good-natured support of my projects.

Introduction

People often refer to the enormous size of Ontario. Travellers driving cross-country will speak in hushed tones of the amount of time spent just making their way across this one province. But I was born and raised in Ontario and so, like the fish not recognizing the importance of water, I'd always taken its enormity for granted—until I came to write this book. The province is huge geographically, but it is also huge in terms of its population and history. I quickly went from a lifetime of taking for granted and blissfully ignoring Ontario's size to almost the opposite—dealing with all the grand implications of it—every day, for a year. The good news was that there was no shortage of potential research material. The bad news was that I sometimes felt totally overwhelmed by the project.

Fortunately, I had another Ontario-based fact working in my favour. There are some pretty terrific people living in the province, and many of them were very helpful to me as I went about tackling the challenge that I'd set out for myself.

This is my fourth book of "true" Canadian ghost stories (after *Ghost Stories of Alberta, More Ghost Stories of Alberta* and *Ghost Stories of Manitoba*). Quite understandably, people often ask me if I'm psychic or have ever seen a ghost. The answer to both those questions is "no." My sole interest in ghost stories is that they combine two of my greatest passions—history and mystery. Ontario's history is lengthy and diverse and, as a result, the province has many ghosts and haunted places—those spectres have created the "mystery" component of the equation.

Defining the term "ghost" would seem like a sensible place to start trying to solve this mystery. Searching out that definition has become something of a mission for me over the past ten years. Along the way, I've also puzzled over the mysteries of "Why are ghosts here?" "Why are some people so much more likely to see a ghost than are others?" and "Why are some places haunted, while others may have seen more traumatic events and yet remain 'cold'?" Nevertheless, I'm not sure that I'm much further ahead now than when I started.

However, I have developed some firm theories as to what a ghost is *not*. A ghost is not a cute, white cartoon character, nor is it a human figure draped in a white sheet. A ghost is also not necessarily a filmy, gauzy apparition, although there certainly are some that fit that description. Frederic Myers, author of *Human Personality and Its Survival of Bodily Death* (1903) and one of the founding members of the old and honourable Society for Psychical Research in England, suggested that a ghost is "an indication that some kind of force is being exercised after death" and that this force "is in some way connected with a person" now deceased. He further purported that ghosts are unaware of themselves and incapable of thought.

With all due respect to the learned Dr. Myers, I wonder whether that last statement is one hundred percent true in all cases of hauntings. Some ghosts seem to only be continuing on about their life's business, completely oblivious to the world of the living that surrounds them. Others, for example "forerunners" (see below), have specific tasks that they are determined to perform, such as delivering a message.

An issue of semantics arises in retelling ghost stories. There are few true synonyms in the English language, and I have chosen to use the following words interchangeably: spectre, spirit, entity, presence, phantom and ghost. Not all ghosts present themselves visually in the shape of humans. Those that do are more properly called "apparitions." However, a ghost may be present only in the form of a sensation—a person feeling that he or she is not alone, although no one else is physically present. Ghosts can also manifest as smells—both pleasant and unpleasant. Other manifestations include ghostly lights and phantom music.

A "poltergeist" is a rare type of spectral being that can be identified by its noisy and possibly violent behaviours. It will often move objects and can actually wreak havoc on its surrounding physical environment. Poltergeists are associated with people rather than places. They have been known to follow people for years, even through a succession of moves. In this book, the story "Bewitched, Cursed or Haunted" (p. 132) contains dramatic examples of poltergeist hauntings.

But why do ghostly phenomena exist? "Leftover energy" (physical or emotional) is a theory used to explain the existence of ghosts. This theory is closely related to the "psychic imprint" proposition—that the essence of a person has somehow been "stamped" onto the environment in which that person lived. The deceased person's soul has effectively left an imprint on the physical world. He or she has become a ghost. Traumatic or violent events can also leave such a mark, resulting in a place being haunted.

Another theory holds that ghosts are disembodied souls (or energies, personalities or spirits) that are usually detectable only by our (nearly atrophied) sixth sense. Rather than perceiving this other-worldly sensation with our currently active and familiar five senses, we may notice the hair on our arms or on the back of our neck standing on end, or a tingling sensation in our skin, or that decidedly disconcerting feeling that we are not alone or that we are being watched. According to some students of the subject, ghosts are beings who either don't know that the body they occupied is deceased or can't accept death because they feel obligated to complete unfinished business among the living.

Throughout all of these suppositions lurks a further mystery: Does the ghost originate with the living person who is experiencing the encounter, or with the ghost itself? Perhaps that point is debatable but, because many people report seeing or sensing the same spirit either at the same or different times, the entity is certainly more objective than merely a figment of "the mind's eye."

A ghost might also be the result of "retrocognition"—seeing or sensing the past. Precognition, of course, is the opposite—seeing or sensing an event that has not yet occurred—and, when such an experience is accompanied by a presence, that presence is called a "forerunner."

Despite the lack of agreement about what a ghost might be, ghosts exist in all cultures and have been noted throughout history. My own experience collecting ghost stories has taught me one other consistency: A paranormal encounter is a profoundly moving experience. I have yet to have a story told to me in a flippant or even matter-of-fact way. Experiencing a ghost is clearly a deeply moving event in a person's life. Out of respect for this emotional factor, I have agreed to protect a contributor's anonymity when he or she has requested that I do so.

Some people are much more likely to encounter a ghost than are others. I have heard the suggestion that some of us are more tuned to the wavelength on which ghosts transmit. Although this sensitivity seems to be inborn, it is also apparent that the ability can be either enhanced or diminished with practice.

Being haunted is not necessarily a permanent status for either person or place. A place that is currently haunted may not always be so. Conversely, just because your home and workplace are now ghost-free zones is no guarantee that they will always remain so.

Some ghosts and hauntings are incredibly tenacious. For example, the ghosts of Roman soldiers are still occasionally spotted roaming the English countryside where they battled centuries ago—but few ghosts are that ancient. As I have never heard or read of any place or person being haunted by the ghost of a "caveman," I presume that, like all forms of energy, ghosts eventually weaken to the point of virtual dissipation.

In the presence of a ghost or during an active haunting, observers will usually note predictable and distinguishable changes in their environment, often including a sudden, dramatic temperature drop that is very localized, though it may encompass a larger area. There may also be drafts or odours or noises—all of which are apparently sourceless.

The ghost stories included in this book are not works of fiction. As a result, they tend to be more ragged than the stories that we're used to reading. A fictional account of a haunting will be structured, with a predictable presentation—a beginning, a middle and an end. The anecdotes recorded here refuse to be that tidy—they are often merely fragments, which can be somewhat frustrating in a world so fond of neatness. We like to have any loose ends bound up by the last sentence—it's more satisfying. But the stories in this book are reports of real events—and we all know that life as we live it is anything but neat and tidy. I consider myself merely a recorder of events and so have resisted the temptation to craft any of the stories to make them conform to an expected standard. I have, by now, come to view the parts of the story-puzzle that are missing as being as provocative as the parts that have remained. Where I have inserted words of clarification within quoted passages, these additions are within square brackets [like this].

This collection is not an attempt to alter anyone's personal belief systems with my convictions or explanations. My intent is to entertain and to possibly provoke thought in areas that you might otherwise not have considered exploring. Though I do not pretend to be an educator, if reading this book introduces you to facets of Ontario's history and geography with which you were previously unfamiliar, then I am delighted.

I have purposely excluded the many Native peoples' tales of spirits and the supernatural. Although these stories would definitely make a fascinating book, I am not qualified to write them.

If you have any additions to the stories contained in this volume, or personal ghost stories that you would like to share with me, please contact me through Lone Pine Publishing. I'd love to hear from you. In the meantime, do enjoy this unique look at some of Ontario's folklore.

Chapter 1

HAUNTED HOUSES

The Old Boyd Place

The Boyd Gang's reign of bank-robbing terror began in the last months of the 1940s and persisted intermittently until 1953. The gang's exploits, as colourfully reported (and frequently embellished upon) in the newspapers, held law-abiding citizens of the day mesmerized. Eddie Boyd, the mob's leader, was not only a dashing Errol Flynn look-alike, but a snappy dresser and a real charmer.

Tragically, the Boyd Gang's crimes escalated until a Toronto police officer was fatally shot. The robbers had gone too far. They were hunted down and arrested. In December of 1953, the two gang members responsible for killing the police officer were executed and the others were sentenced to varying lengths of incarceration. But in the court of public opinion, Eddie Boyd had attained a degree of folk-hero status, a position he retained for many years.

Bob and Heike Murdoch, along with their son and daughter, live in Severn Bridge, a Muskoka-area town that Bob describes as consisting of a tavern, a variety store, an auto repair shop, a marina and about 250 souls. He lives in a century-old home built by Eddie Boyd's uncle, Andrew.

Bob's been told that the gang hid out on this land on more than one occasion. Given that members of the Boyd Gang were known to have sought sanctuary with relatives when they were in need of hideouts, it is quite possible that what Bob has been led to believe is entirely true.

Since 1986, when the Murdochs purchased the two-storey house, they may have wondered occasionally whether or not they had bought more than they bargained for. On the plus side, there might be money buried somewhere on the property, but balancing that tantalizing possibility is the reality that the place is very haunted. While the possible buried treasure would presumably be a Boyd Gang legacy, the ghosts are probably not.

Oddly, Bob Murdoch felt driven to buy the house some three years before it was actually put up for sale. "I was drawn to it like a magnet. For some reason I was meant to buy this old place. When I first saw it I was compelled to get it."

When the property came into Bob's life once again, he reports, "I bought it without seeing it inside [but] from the first minute I walked into the place it was familiar to me."

A great deal of work needed to be done to the house before the Murdoch family could move in, and they began the necessary tasks at once. Ghosts are often provoked by renovations to "their" abode. Bob's first-ever ghostly encounter in the haunted house proved that point.

"During the rebuilding...I lay down for a small power-nap in the mid-afternoon. When I woke up there was an old woman standing at the end of my little day bed. She was a large-boned woman with her hair done up in a bun on the back and top of her head. She wore a common full-length dress with a full-length apron, frills on the shoulders—nothing fancy, very practical. She had her fists planted firmly on her hips. She was studying the large barn beams I had just put up as if she was trying to make up her mind if she approved. She was enveloped in a purple haze that moved like smoke would move but it stayed around her. She looked me in the eye, seemed to approve then drifted away up the stairs."

The comment "if these walls could talk" is frequently made about an old place. In Bob Murdoch's case, it was not the walls but the floors that effectively communicated a story to him. On the floor at one end of the dining room, where table would reasonably have been, the planks were nearly disintegrated,

This very haunted, century-old house was constructed by Andrew Boyd, uncle of the infamous bank robber Eddie Boyd.

"by what could only have been hobnail boots. I presume the father was at one end of the table and a son or boarder was at the other end and they were too lazy or didn't have enough respect for the house or the lady that tried to best take care of it, to take their boots off when they came home for supper."

Bob continued, "The lady who lived here, however, did love the place, I think. The most prolific bunch of roses, tiger lilies, morning glories and gladiolas came back to life all over the front yard after I cut the weeds back. There were other things I found as I was working around in the house that showed somebody cared as well. Pieces of colourful cloth glued to the walls, etc. I like to think it was the woman in the lavender haze."

This spirit may have been responsible for saving the house and its occupants from a potentially lethal fire. Bob had designed a creative heating system for the house, one that operates simply and safely once all the components are properly in place. One night, some time after midnight, Bob awoke suddenly from a deep sleep.

"I sat bolt upright in bed just as though someone gave me a slap right alongside the head. Immediately, before I realized what I was doing, I was halfway down the stairs."

The man puzzled over his actions only for a moment before noticing that the heater door was wide open, not bolted closed as it should have been. The additional air that the open door had let in caused the fire in the well stoked stove to develop to a dangerous level, just short of being out of control.

Quickly rectifying the potentially dangerous problem, Bob pondered his sudden awakening and seemingly thoughtless rush to the kitchen "What woke me up?" he wondered. "It was like someone gave me a slap. Was the little old lady upstairs waking me up? What was she doing? I don't know, but it's always been a question in my mind."

Perhaps the former occupant is pleased that once again someone's taking care of "her" old house and she's merely doing what she can to support the efforts.

An elderly neighbour of the Murdochs has told Bob and Heike she remembers as a little girl being told not to go near the Boyd house when a certain individual was visiting there. This man was noted for playing especially vicious and potentially dangerous pranks. The neighbour recalled that the man once put a rattlesnake in the wood box. Bob wonders if it was the spirit of that mean man who helped to create a second dangerous incident concerning the stoves.

"In the mornings...I take a shovel full of coals out of the [heating] stove and put them in the cookstove to get it going," Bob explained. "This particular day...I was walking across to put [the coals] into the cookstove. My wife was standing there watching me and for some reason the coals just went up in the air and down on the floor. I didn't say anything to Heike. I was just kicking myself in the butt for being so clumsy and yet I was saying to myself, 'I didn't DO that.'" Bob recalled. "My wife was still looking at me. She said, 'You didn't dump those things. I watched. You stumbled over something but there's nothing there. Your foot tripped on something but there's nothing there.'"

Bob had to agree with Heike's assessment of what had just happened.

"I said to myself, she's right. I didn't drop them. Maybe it was this prankster who put the rattlesnake in the wood box."

If so, the cruel practical joker may also have caused another accident in the kitchen.

"I was making breakfast for the kids and rather than wait for the wood stove I just put the kettle on the electric stove. It's a big kettle. I'd say about a four-litre chrome kettle. It was boiling and I wanted to put it on the end of the counter. I was going to make the kids' porridge with it and as I turned [the kettle] just went sideways down onto the floor and burned my foot real bad; second and third degree burns. It happened so quick. I came back [from having the burns attended to] and I'm thinking about it and I realize this is really strange. I didn't drop that kettle. I'm not a weak individual. I can carry a bucket of water and [yet] this thing just went right out of my hand," Bob continued, trying to puzzle out the series of events that had transpired. "I inspected the kettle. It's got a dent on the side of it where it hit the floor. I went through the motions myself. I got it full of water. If I let go of it, it should go straight down and land

on its bottom [but] it had landed on its side. I was playing the
episode over in my mind after the fact. I remember that kettle
hitting something as I came across to put it on the table. That
space there is about three feet wide and about a foot away from
anything but still the kettle went down sideways, which meant it
had to turn in my hand in order for it to land on its side on the
floor. It would have actually had to turn in mid-air...which
means something hit it and knocked it sideways, reached it out
of my hand, threw it on the floor and the resulting splash burned
my foot."

Despite these isolated instances, the Murdochs continued to
enjoy living in their home.

"With the exception of an upstairs window, I felt very
comfortable in [the house]. Whenever I came near that window I
got the feeling I was standing in someone else's space."

Through the twelve years Bob has called the house home, this
strange feeling has not changed.

"The window I feel uncomfortable with is a simple single-
hung window that faces west from the top of the staircase. The
feeling I get, as I said, is as though I was standing in someone
else's space and they would like me to move back a little, but
along with this feeling I have also had the impression sometimes
that the individual's space I'm standing in is somehow crippled,
or in a wheelchair. I don't know why I get this impression but the
feeling is quite strong."

A guest experienced similar feelings in that same spot. At the
time when the young man expressed this reaction, he had no idea
anyone else had ever felt that way in that particular spot.

Heike Murdoch endured a series of dreams that might also be
connected with this presence.

"The scenes of her dream go from seeing a woman at the top
of the stairs one minute as though in a tense conversation with

someone. Heike saw the expression on the woman's face but she couldn't see what was going on. Then the next scene is [the woman] appearing unconscious at the bottom of the stairs in a heap. As her dream [continued over a series of nights,] she came closer and closer to seeing what caused [the woman] to fall, but she never really [saw] what or who it is," Bob related, before adding his own insight. "I put myself in the position of the victim. If the spirit of the poor woman was trying to tell my wife she was pushed, it would be very possible then that the only impression she could convey to my wife was the accident itself, because she maybe didn't know who pushed her either."

Heike's feelings that the woman in her dream was somehow physically disabled supported a sensation that Bob had wondered about. That area had often made him think of someone being trapped in some way.

The first years the Murdochs lived in Andrew Boyd's old place were busy ones for the new owners. One of the major projects to be tackled was the installation of a septic system in the backyard.

"While we were digging we found bones, human bones, the bones of two children. The police say [the skeletons] were older than fifty years so they didn't care about them, but somebody cared because sometimes at night we can hear children's voices as they play. I can never make out what they are saying but I know they are voices because I can hear the pitch rise and fall and the sounds of laughter coming from what we call 'the haunted room' [see below]. Whenever I got up to go and see, the sounds would stop."

The previous occupant of the house confirmed Bob's experiences, with only one rather interesting difference. When Bob hears the sounds of children's voices and laughter, it sounds to him as though the noises emanate from inside the house. But, says Bob, "The lady who lived here before us also heard the children, although she thought she heard the sounds coming from outside."

The haunted room has an interesting story. Bob continued, "When my daughter was still living here, I built her a loft bedroom in [the] area of the house that gave me [the] anxious feeling. It was very dilapidated and had been used for storing nothing of value it would seem, but the door had a padlock clasp on it. I found this odd because there weren't locks on any of the other interior doors. The area had not been used in quite some time so it's hard to say if anyone had lived in it or not."

Bob noted that his daughter "slept there for about a month and refused to stay there any more. On more than one occasion she complained of waking up with the feeling of having someone sitting on top of her. On the last night [that] she endured the feeling it felt as though something was holding her down by the arms then [lying] with its full weight flat out on top of her making it hard for her [to] breathe. She struggled out from underneath it and ran downstairs to sleep on the couch," Bob continued. He added, "No one has used the loft since."

Bob and Heike had to find alternative accommodation for their daughter. They chose a small upstairs room, one the family has since come to consider as central to the haunting. In typical teenage-girl fashion, Bob's daughter became extremely fond of her bedroom. Because this fondness is such a common phenomenon, the Murdochs paid little attention to the girl's attachment to the room, except to note that she had mentioned enjoying "nice dreams in vivid colour" while sleeping there.

"We never really paid too much attention...until she moved out...[then] we couldn't keep the door closed. If I closed and latched the door it would be open again in the morning.... My wife chose not to believe it could be the voices that opened the door. [O]ne night just before she was going out we almost argued about it. Our voices got higher and higher. I was saying that there was definitely something in that room and she was saying, 'no there isn't, there's nothing there and I don't want to hear any more about it,' and she left. She came back home late that night, about two in the morning. She walked up the stairs to come to bed and, as she walked past the haunted room, as though the occupant of the room was trying to convince her there was more to it than she was willing to believe, the latch moved. She looked, then she saw the latch lift and the door open. She stopped, reached for the door and heard an ominous shuffle of feet on the other side of the door. She shut the door and ran into the bedroom to me. We were the only ones home at the time."

That experience no doubt ruined any of Heike's attempts at skepticism, for it is now the room they consider to be haunted by not only the old woman but also the phantom children. At least one of those immature spirits had a terrific time after a birthday party for the Murdochs' son in the early 1990s.

The party itself was not held in their haunted house but in an (apparently) unhaunted restaurant. The celebration was a huge success, complete with birthday cake and balloons. No doubt most of the cake was eaten at the party, but the balloons survived well and the family took them home afterward.

"They were filled with helium and floated up to the ceiling. The one aluminum [metallized mylar] balloon stayed up while the other ones dropped down after losing some helium. The next night the aluminum balloon was still flying high—up to the ceiling in the living room. By the time everyone was ready for bed the balloon had drifted over to the staircase and drifted upstairs. It was resting against the ceiling right above the staircase when I went up to bed. I pushed the long colourful ribbons that trailed down from the balloon out of my way as I went by them."

Bob continued, "My wife was in the upstairs washroom and I went into our bedroom across from where the balloon was resting. The balloon went down the hall under another door header into my son's room, across his room to a back window, then stopped and 'looked' out the back window for a period of time. While I was standing there, the balloon drifted to our bedroom. It dipped down to get under the door header, then continued past me so close [that] my breath would have moved it, had I breathed on it. It stopped at [a] little...window that looks out on the front lawn. While I was standing there, my wife came out of the bathroom and entered the bedroom. The balloon drifted back across the room under the door header, across his room and stopped at a small window that looks out on to the backyard."

Aghast at the controlled movements he'd been watching an inanimate object perform, Bob Murdoch asked his wife, "Did you see that?" Although Heike certainly had been witness to the balloon's strange movements, she attributed them to air currents coming through a nearby open window. Bob had to agree that there was something of a breeze in the room, but he had noticed a minute detail about the way the balloon moved.

"It's not the wind," he countered. "Look at the ribbons."

As he began to explain the oddity he'd noticed, the balloon demonstrated exactly the point he was trying to make.

"[It] continued past us under the haunted room's door header and stopped at a small window looking out to the side yard. If it was the wind blowing the balloon along, the balloon would go first and the ribbons would follow. Instead, the ribbons were going first, pulling the balloon along [as if] by an unseen hand."

Perhaps the little child-ghost who'd missed so many of his or her own birthday parties was merely playing with one of the toys remaining from Bob's son's party. The Murdochs thoroughly enjoyed having such an enchanting and whimsical paranormal event take place in their beloved home.

Heike has always cherished the sense of security the old house gives her, especially during severe weather. As Bob so colourfully put it, "Knowing its weathered walls have stood the storms of many years, she can bask in the glowing warmth of a comfortable wood fire, secure and warm in the face of nature's rage."

On one particular winter's night, she was not the only presence enjoying the refuge of the house.

Bob explained, "...my wife couldn't sleep. She curled up on a couch downstairs with a book and the soothing warmth of the old wood stove. It was one of those midwinter nights when the temperature falls to thirty below, when the wind assumes a life of its own, whipping snow into tiny whirlwinds, driving them across the fields like dancing devils [and] then burying them in drifts and piles by the tree line."

Bob continued, "She had been reading in sublime comfort for some time when she heard that upstairs bedroom door open and a shuffle of feet make [their] way to the head of the stairs. She looked over her shoulder and up the stairs expecting to see me but saw nothing. She looked across the room in front of her where the cat was also trying to see what was moving down the stairs. She turned back to the stairs and felt a gentle cold draft pass down behind her. At a point when the draft would be just past her almost to the last stair, a great blast of icy wind exploded in from the kitchen as though the woodshed door had been blown open by the raging wind-beasts outside."

Bob's wife had to find out what had caused this sudden wind. "My wife and the cat jumped up and ran into the kitchen. The whole place was icy cold. The blast of air was over. The house was in dead silence again and, much to her surprise, the woodshed door was still closed. She was astounded by the sudden ferocity of the experience with no apparent reason for it but she simply picked up the cat and returned to the couch, her book and the warmth of the wood stove. Even though the wood stove was still going full blast, both the kitchen and the living room were too cold to sit in so, in her words, 'If the ghosts want to party for the night then to hell with them. I'm going to bed.' And so she did."

Bob always wondered if his accidents with the burning coals and the boiling water, as well as his wife's experience with the sudden, unexplainable blast of cold air, were in some way connected to two frightening sightings.

The Murdochs' son is now a university student and is away from home for most of the year. When he was home during a school break during the winter of 1997, Bob's wife had an encounter she'll not soon forget.

She got up from bed in the middle of the night. "As she looked down the stairs from the landing she saw what she thought was our son standing at the bottom. She called out, 'Why are you up so late?' With that, she looked a little closer and suddenly realized [that] what was standing at the bottom of the stairs [was] about the size of our son [but] had no head, or no face, she's not quite sure now, but she was quite sure it wasn't our son. As she watched, the vision just vanished."

Now it was Bob's turn to be skeptical—that is, until about one month later.

"My son had gone back to school. A man who worked for me at the time, and I, were coming home late after a long job. There was a lot of snow on the ground and the air was cold. We said goodbye in the yard and he went to his car. I heard his car running outside and was making myself a cup of tea when he came running into the house and asked if I was just outside behind his car. I said, 'no.' He told me he saw what he thought was me standing behind his car and he waited for me to get out of the way. When it seemed like I wasn't about to move he said he got out of the car and told me to get out of the way so he could go home. As he was talking to what he thought was me he realized it had no face. Then as he watched, it disappeared. The description of what he saw was exactly the same as what my wife said she saw. He was so disturbed by this [event that] he had his sister make me a spirit/dream catcher and made me hang it up in the kitchen. I must admit since we hung it up we haven't really had many odd occurrences."

Bob paused for a moment before adding a surprise ending to the story: "We find it lonesome in here now with the spirit catcher. I'm thinking of taking it down just to see what would happen."

The spirit catcher hanging from the ceiling lamp has put an end to the ghostly appearances—for now.

Marley

Candy Alexander lives in a 150-year-old house just west of Prescott. Considering the age of the place, it's rather amazing that it hasn't had many owners, but the Alexanders are only the fourth occupants. It seems that anyone who buys this particular house stays in it for a minimum of twenty years. Such stability usually doesn't lead to a haunting but, for a period of years, the Alexanders clearly shared their beautifully located real estate with a ghost—a ghost they named Marley.

Given that Marley liked to socialize with the Alexanders and apparently even partied occasionally without them, he might be a remnant from somewhere between the late 1800s and the 1920s, when Wiser's Distillery owned the property. If he is, then it's odd that he never manifested himself to the woman who lived in the house immediately after the distillery moved on to new premises. Even today, that former owner takes great pleasure in coming back to visit her old home, and Candy, at least twice a year. The two women have come to know one another well over the years. Candy reports that she enjoys being entertained by the older woman's many stories, but that those stories never include a reference to the house being haunted.

However, the Alexanders were made amply aware of their ghost. They thoroughly enjoyed relaxing around the fireplace in their ground-floor family room and they'd always know when Marley joined them there. "The unattended rocking chair would begin to rock and continue [doing] so for a few minutes."

Occasionally, Marley must have considered Candy and Doug's company insufficient. At least once, while relaxing by herself at a time when she was not expecting company, Candy has heard the sounds of cars pulling up outside the house. Next would come the sound of car doors closing, and so the woman naturally would presume that unexpected company had arrived. She would make her way to the yard to greet friends, but there would never be anyone there. The couple soon came to accept that when they heard these phantom sounds, "Marley was having a party with his ghostly friends."

One of those ghostly get-togethers must have gotten a bit out of hand, for Candy noted that her "[riding] lawn tractor, which used to be just outside the kitchen window, was found one morning turned 180 degrees from its original position."

The current kitchen, adjacent to the family room, is another spot where Marley has played his phantom pranks.

"[A] dish or glass would gently 'fall' from the drying rack onto the kitchen floor and land upright with no damage."

Animals are almost always more aware of presences than are humans. When the Alexanders had guests who brought their cats along, the humans were given a dramatic demonstration of this phenomenon.

"The cats would freak—particularly when [they were] in the second of two bedrooms. Their fur would just stand literally straight up for as long as they were up there," Candy recalled.

Gord Alexander's sister Ruth and her husband, Doug Butcher, were given a most impressive show of this phenomenon. They arrived for a visit once just in time to see a terrified cat "come out of an open basement window shrieking with its fur standing straight up."

Fortunately for the Alexanders and their visiting friends, family and pets, Marley's methods were not always so sensational. He could even be subtle when he wanted to be. Ruth and Doug Butcher remember "articles left on a coffee table in the evening would be in a different location the next morning."

Candy Alexander's haunted house as it looked in 1927 and then again in 1987, when Marley the ghost was in residence.

Since those days of frenetic phantom activity, Marley now seems to have vanished. Candy explained that opinion is split on the circumstances of his departure.

"In 1992 we finally finished redecorating on the bedroom level. [S]hortly after we finished varnishing the two bedroom doors, we looked and, believe it or not, there is quite a visible 'man' stuck on the door. He is rather thin, wearing a very narrow tie. Perhaps it is the demise of Marley because since then there have been no more apparent 'ghostly' behaviour[s]."

Doug Butcher wonders if Marley didn't decide to retire in Florida.

"Gordie and Candy came to visit us in Florida and stayed overnight. Some time later, after they had left, two nights in succession at *exactly* [emphasis Doug's] the same time (4:45 a.m.), the toilet seat fell for no apparent reason. We had returned to Ontario and after they had visited our trailer in a park a battery-operated alarm clock (from which the batteries had been removed) went off two mornings in a row at exactly the same time—5 a.m. These occurrences we blamed on Marley, whom we jokingly said had been left behind by Gordie and Candy."

As the trip to Florida and the varnished doors happened at about the same time, it's hard to tell. All Candy Alexander knows for sure is that her house is no longer haunted by Marley the "party animal."

Herbie

Ted and Suzanne Currie are well-educated, down-to-earth people. Suzanne earns her living as a teacher and Ted, a former newspaper editor, now freelances. Despite their decidedly pragmatic natures, Ted readily acknowledged, "We're receptive to wayward spirits...we've had some dandies."

One occurrence in particular stands out in the Curries' minds. "Herbie," as they named the little wraith, came into their lives shortly after they moved to a bungalow within commuting distance of Bracebridge.

"It was beautifully situated, across from Lake Muskoka, amidst huge evergreens at the front and an enormous tract of forest directly behind. There were neighbours on both sides, similar cottage-type abodes, simple structures that began as uninsulated cottages in the 1940s and were then insulated and added on to over the years to accommodate year-round occupancy," Ted described.

They moved to this idyllic setting in the autumn of 1987, when their first son, Andrew, was two. Their second son, Robert, was born not long after they settled in. In retrospect, they suspect that Andrew was the first family member to become aware of the ghost.

"Before Robert was born, Andrew had experienced his first episode of what we came to believe was 'night terror.' His room faced the backyard and was the smallest of the three bedrooms," Ted explained, before adding that the child's bedroom directly across from their bedroom, which faced the lake. "Andrew would wake up any time from 1:30 a.m. to 2:30 a.m. crying and sick to his stomach. It happened on numerous occasions. That autumn we took him to the family doctor to investigate...the problem."

The physician's diagnosis aligned with the Curries' thoughts of night terrors, which Ted understood as being "a common, although disturbing circumstance for youngsters."

Ted continued, "Some time later that winter, while watching the Mary Martin version of *Peter Pan*...Andrew became quite upset about a face in the window...in his room. He asked whether the face he saw was Peter Pan trying to get into the house. At first we thought it was just a negative reaction on his part to Peter Pan, [perhaps] wishing not to follow him to 'Never-Never Land.' Eventually, however, we started to put the pieces together and found a strong relationship between Andrew's 'night terror' and seeing the face in the window or at least being stirred from sleep by something."

In order to establish that this was a change in behaviour for the little boy, Ted explained, "Before moving to the lakeside house, Andrew had been sleeping through the night. Once in that rear bedroom in our new home, he seldom slept through [the whole night] and several nights each week he would also be sick to his stomach."

Not knowing what else to do, the Curries tried assigning Andrew a new bedroom. "We finally decided to change bed-rooms and place Andrew in the lake-facing bedroom down the hall...still only steps from our bedroom. From the time we moved Andrew [to the new bedroom], by midwinter 1988, the 'night terrors' ceased. In fact, he never had a similar episode and to this day we wonder about the face that apparently stared through the bedroom window. Peter Pan? Imagination? Text-book night terror?"

The questions are rhetorical because, as Ted concluded, "Andrew doesn't remember much about the occurrences now but isn't fond of *Peter Pan*, which hasn't been viewed from our video library since that year."

Just because the entity was no longer disturbing their son's sleep didn't mean that the couple was sure it was gone entirely.

"It was in August of 1988 that Suzanne had her first encounter with our ghostly lodger, possibly the little boy responsible for frightening Andrew those many nights that previous autumn and winter," Ted Currie continued. "In our open-concept living room–kitchen, Suzanne was working at an island counter stove, facing the front picture window and the door to the outside deck. It was about 4 p.m. and she was preparing dinner and I was sitting on the deck while our boys were playing in the circular drive directly in front. Andrew was on his tricycle and Robert was playing in the sand with a toy truck. Our dog Alf was sitting on the walkway watching the boys at play. At one point I remember looking overtop [of] my newspaper because the din of youngsters playing had been, for whatever reason, silenced. Both boys and the dog were staring intently into the house, through the wedged-open front door. It looked odd but I assumed they were watching Suzanne, possibly coming out with cookies and glasses of lemonade. I put my paper down and actually anticipated a cold beverage. The boys never stopped glaring into the house but Suzanne didn't come out."

Perhaps slightly disappointed at not receiving the drink that he'd been expecting, Ted went back to his newspaper. "Halfway through another story…Suzanne arrived on the deck, the colour drained from her cheeks, in an obvious state of shock. I asked what was wrong."

Suzanne was all too ready to explain, "Did you see something a minute ago?" she began.

"Such as?" inquired Ted.

"I think I've seen a ghost!" she declared in a raspy voice. "A little boy ran in through the door right up to the counter and then disappeared."

Suzanne was so unnerved by her experience that she couldn't continue. Instead, she stepped down from the deck where she'd been talking to Ted and picked up Robert from the sandy driveway.

"She stood for a few minutes looking back into the house, anticipating the wee lad to make a second appearance."

Wherever the spectre was, he was by now no longer visible, for neither adult could see anything out of the ordinary, and their sons and the family dog had gone back to what they'd been doing before anyone had detected the presence.

Suzanne told Ted, "I was working at the stove, facing the front door. I turned around to get something from the sink and when I arrived back at the stove I glanced up and saw the young boy, about seven years old, I would guess, running into the house. He was waving his arms, as a child dances and runs at the same time. He had dirty blonde hair that appeared windblown, quite long, and I watched him from the doorway right to the bookshelf in front of the stove where I was working. Then he just vanished. His face was just a blur. It was his actions that were so memorable. The flailing arms and flying hair. Like he was excited and was coming into the house to relay some information. And then—[he was] gone. Without a trace," Suzanne added.

"It really frightened me. It was so unexpected. Here I am making dinner and all of a sudden there's a boy we don't know, running through the house. After awhile I adjusted. Probably just my imagination," she concluded in an attempt to reconcile the event.

Suzanne Currie didn't have much time to let that rationalization set comfortably in her head when she saw the image again.

"I had something on the stove and had my head down. [I saw] the same wild hair, blondish. He was without a shirt and he was dirty—as if he had been playing in the sand. Just after a glimpse of him, standing within a few feet, he vanished again. Actually in the same spot as the afternoon before," she explained.

Suzanne was understandably thrown by her encounter and felt somewhat fearful of the image. Although there were no further sightings of the ghostly lad, Suzanne has been made aware of his presence, "with a shiver, many other times."

Despite a time lapse of more than ten years, the apparition's appearance has remained clear in her mind.

"I can see him as clearly today as I did on those two occasions," she confesses in a casual recollection. "I felt that somehow this child was lost, confused and may have thought, if ghosts can [think], that I was his mother. Possibly this had been his home at some point and he became separated from his family. I'm not eager to see him again. It was a frightening experience when one minute you're working on making dinner and the next you're staring at, well, possibly a wayward spirit."

Suzanne's sightings, followed by her sense that the little wraith was near, although not visible, made his spirit very real to the Curries—real enough that they needed to name him. Suzanne chose to call the lost soul "Herbie." The couple wondered if their sons had seen the manifestation, but chose not to probe.

For a time they were left with the mystery, but an experience of Ted's led the couple to at least a partial explanation.

"Later that summer I had a strange experience that didn't involve a sighting [like] my wife witnessed but arrived in a dream. It was in late August. It was a beautiful later summer evening that was warm enough to swim, wear shorts and stay out on the deck...late at night. Suzanne was outside with our boys on the deck. I decided to have a short nap in the master bedroom. I don't know how long I was asleep but it wasn't much beyond an hour. I awoke when I heard a tremendous crash, tires squealing and then the sound of a child screaming. I jumped up and looked out the window believing one of the boys had been hit by a car. I yelled out to Suzanne who then jumped off the deck with Robert in her arms, to see what was wrong. I asked where Andrew was. No sooner had I finished the sentence than Andrew drove his trike up behind Suzanne, also wondering what his dad was so upset about."

Ted asked his wife, "Did you hear a crash?"

"No," Suzanne responded. "Not a thing."

"I could have sworn I heard a car hit a bicycle. Were any of the boys crying just a minute ago?" Ted continued.

"No!" came Suzanne's most emphatic reply.

Finally realizing that the experience had happened solely to him, Ted began to calm down.

"I guess, like Andrew, I had my own 'night terror.' It took a long time to calm down. I was sure a tragedy had occurred," Ted admitted.

It was fully a year later before they were able to get any closure on their experiences.

"Suzanne and I talked to a lady who had lived [down] the road for quite a number of years, who recalled a youngster being struck by a car and subsequently dying from [the] injuries [that he] received. She believed the youngster had been a male, about eight years of age and that he had resided in a home close to ours," Ted said. He went on to add that after that conversation with the lady, "We heard this story from other residents in the years since we moved [from that house] in August 1989."

No more is known about the mysterious little manifestation, and the Curries concluded by acknowledging that they "have no idea whether the new owners experienced this wayward spirit or not. But he certainly made an impression on the Currie family during those brief and curious encounters."

A Presence in the Pantry

Ivy Elliott's fine penmanship would probably reveal a lot to someone trained in graphology. To me, it merely meant that her letter was a pleasure to read. Of course, since it described a personally experienced ghost story, it was an even further delight to me. Mrs. Elliott is now a grandmother living in Orillia, but her story dated back to the 1920s, when she lived in Toronto.

"I was six years old. My parents and [their] three children had not long been in Canada after immigrating from Wales. Things were pretty bad financially...but...they eventually [found] a little house they could afford. It was [on] Fulton Avenue in Toronto. The house had two floors with a long hallway from the front door to the kitchen in the back with stairs going up in the hall. Under the stairs was sort of a pantry off the kitchen," my correspondent recalled.

The pantry was just an empty, closed-in space. There were no shelves in it, nor was there a light switch.

"Just three bare walls, a bare ceiling and the door," Ivy Elliott continued, before explaining that the pantry door did have a knothole, a little over two centimetres around, in it.

"The room opposite this pantry was used by my mother and dad as a bedroom. Dad would always close the bedroom door but during the night the door would creak open and they would see a light shining through the knothole. He would pick up the first thing he could lay his hands on and throw it at [the door] and [then] race to open the pantry door—just to find—nothing at all," she remembers her parents explaining.

But if the phantom light from the pantry had been the only indication that all was not normal in the family's new home, Ivy's parents might have been able to accept it.

"Other nights the [bedroom] door would open and it was just as though someone or something jumped on the bottom of the bed and the bed would bounce up and down. They would be up out of bed in a shot, nerves on edge, but nothing was to be seen."

The mystery of the strange activities in the house continued until Ivy's older sister made friends with another youngster in the neighbourhood. This girl's young brother had died by drowning in a well on the property where Ivy and her family now lived. The man who owned the house at the time of the tragedy was so overwhelmed by the accident that he had hanged himself—in the pantry.

Ivy remembered that her family had moved on not too long after learning of this probable explanation for the haunting of their first Canadian home. They heard some time later that the family who had moved in after them had once "fled into the street in their night clothes."

She ended her story by telling me that she now enjoys retelling that and other tales from her childhood to her grandchildren, "who listen with wide eyes and open mouths and beg to be told again and again," the story of the haunted house.

"You're in the Haunted House"

The gentleman who told me this haunted house story asked that he be referred to by the pseudonym "W.A. Luvlake." His actual identity is on file in his letter, which also asserts that, before the incidents enumerated here occurred, he was a complete skeptic.

In June 1976, Mr. Luvlake, his (now ex-) wife and three children moved to a large house, which he described as being located in southwestern Ontario, roughly halfway between Mount Brydges and Strathroy, on Highway 81. As the family was new to the area, they began to introduce themselves to their new neighbours. Whenever they explained to anyone which house it was they'd moved to, the reply would be, "Oh, you're in the haunted house." Though these comments were no doubt somewhat unnerving, it at least prepared them for what was ahead.

The house had two staircases, one of which had been sealed off. The master bedroom was on the main floor. The children slept upstairs, where there was also an unheated storage room. Once the colder weather came, all three children began complaining about how cold it was in their bedrooms. It didn't take Luvlake long to figure out why his kids were becoming uncomfortable during the night—the door to the back storage area was open.

The father closed the door firmly and left instructions with the youngsters that they were not to open it. All three protested that they had not opened the door previously and had no intention of ever doing so, but the storage room door was always open when they woke up in the morning.

"I got fed up and put a hook and eye on it to be sure it stayed closed and considered that the end of the problem. Not so [for] then the noise started. This storeroom was directly above the kitchen area and usually after darkness, when [all the family members] were downstairs, it would sound as though someone were walking around [upstairs]," Luvlake recalled.

Because Luvlake was not only a skeptic but also away working a great deal of the time, he remembers not taking his family's tales of phantom footsteps at all seriously—that is, not until one evening that he was alone in the house sitting at the kitchen table reading the newspaper.

"All of a sudden I heard this *clomp, clomp* like someone in work boots [was walking on the floor] above me," the man said.

Thinking that his son had returned home and had decided to play a practical joke on his skeptical father, Luvlake set out to search the house and foil the boy. Unfortunately, the man was not able to carry out his plan, for the lad was innocent of any pranks. He was not even home. The boy, his siblings and their mother arrived home some time after Luvlake had heard the clomping sounds. The man's firmly entrenched skepticism had already begun to be eroded away by the unexplainable sounds of footsteps from an empty second floor. The phantom steps were heard intermittently for months after.

In order to make the house both safer and more convenient, Luvlake decided to open up the boarded-over staircase. Those two aims were certainly accomplished, but the renovation had a surprise fringe benefit: it seemed to calm the pacing entity, for the footsteps were no longer heard.

Unfortunately, by that time another door—the door to an outside shed—was giving the family trouble. "If the kids went to put their bikes away or if I was carrying something heavy requiring both hands and went to go in there—*bam*—the door would slam shut right in our faces. No wind, no explanation of any sort."

That particular mystery was never solved. The family members learned to work around it. "I used to prop [the door] open and it took two kids to put bikes away."

The Luvlakes were never able to determine who the ghost was or why it was haunting the house. They moved on after living with a nuisance of a ghost for roughly three years. Mr. Luvlake ended his letter by assuring me that although he had lived in many houses in southwestern Ontario, he'd "never had such an experience again."

A Possessed Manor

There was a stone manor in the Ottawa Valley that was so haunted that it seemed almost totally possessed. The history of the haunting goes back so far that few people could remember a time when the spooky old place was not home to a ghost.

Originally, the house was owned by widowed sisters. The first of the two women to die succumbed to a rather freak accident. Shortly after, the remaining sister simply vanished.

A woman named Mary lives in a house nearby. A visitor she'd been expecting mistakenly arrived at the manor house thinking that it was Mary's place. Wondering whether she'd found the right house, the guest approached the woman she saw sitting on a rocking chair to ask if her friend was there. The woman gave no response. She did not even indicate that she was aware of the visitor's presence. She merely continued to stare straight ahead.

Mary's friend soon realized that she had tried to communicate with a ghost.

One winter night, Mary and her family watched as a dark figure in a hooded robe walked along a path by their home. The family's pet dog appeared to be walking with the figure. The next morning they followed the route where they'd seen the cloaked manifestation and were disturbed to note that there was only one set of footprints in the snow—their dog's.

There were also numerous unexplained injuries associated with the old place. People who'd never been accident-prone often required medical attention after being on the haunted property and suffering accidental injuries. The most dramatic injury occurred just after the Second World War, when a returning sailor decided to show the neighbouring girls how brave he'd become while serving King and country. In his show of bravado, he approached the haunted house after dark. He didn't get very far before he was felled by some unseen force. The young man struggled up and away from the house. His friends took him to the hospital, where he was treated for severe burns.

The next day his friends searched the area where the sailor had been for clues as to what might have burned the young man. The only evidence they found was an old tin that used to hold powdered mustard—the kind of mustard strong enough that it was traditionally used to make hot packs in the days before electric heating pads were readily available.

The evil house manor house was torn down in the early 1980s. No doubt there were few, if any, in the area who mourned its demise.

The Small Ghost

There is no doubt that a paranormal encounter of any kind is a profoundly moving event for the person experiencing it. Fortunately, people's lives are usually only upset for a short time. When the effect is longer lasting, the changes are often viewed as improvements, as positive changes in outlook or ways of thinking. Folks touched in this way generally welcome the increased awareness that an experience with another dimension has made in their lives.

Occasionally, seeing or sensing a spirit can devastate the witness. This effect was the case for Hilda Weiss, a woman who once might have counted herself as a very fortunate person— right up to the day her employer, theatre magnate Ambrose Small, mysteriously vanished (see "Grand Ghosts," p. 74).

Hilda was employed as a maid in the Small household in the tony Toronto community of Rosedale. Both Hilda and the Smalls' chauffeur at the time were sure that Small's ghost was, at least occasionally, present in his former home. They were convinced they heard ghostly noises throughout the nights.

There were many people who suspected that Theresa Small, Ambrose's wife, was responsible for the man's disappearance. They were sure she had murdered the man and buried his body beneath the basement floor of their large home. To add to that frightening thought was the domestic staff's familiarity with an oddity about that basement. It contained all the signs and symbols of the Catholic Church, an important institution in Theresa Small's life, as well as two rooms that remained locked at all times. After her husband's disappearance, Mrs. Small carried the only keys to those chambers with her at all times, and she never went down to the basement of the house unless she was carrying her rosary.

Convinced that the house had become evil and that the restless spirit of her former employer floated about, Hilda Weiss could not endure working in the Small house any longer. She quit, reporting, "It was all so scary. I finally left because I was afraid to spend another night in the place."

The whereabouts of Hilda's employer has never been determined. It is certainly hoped, though, that the frightened maid was able not only to recapture her serenity, but to find another job in a residence that would forever remain unhaunted.

Ghost at Grandma's

John and his brothers are fond of their grandmother—it's her house that makes them uncomfortable.

This particular haunting is a well-established one dating back many years. John's mother remembered that as a child she skipped over the second last step on the stairway, where the family had seen the apparition of a woman, sitting there rocking back and forth.

The entity certainly has a strong personality, complete with a ghostly sense of justice. One day in the late 1980s, John was teasing his preschool-aged brother. He'd taken a toy belonging to the younger boy and was taunting the child by running all over the house with it. John's sense of older-brother-superiority was dashed when he realized that, while playing the game, he had accidentally lost the brand-new sunglasses that he'd had tucked into the waistband of his shorts.

He stopped the chase immediately, gave his little brother back the toy and began to hunt for his missing sunglasses. Initially he was not too concerned about the loss. After all, he hadn't been outside, but rather had been following a specific route in the house. The sunglasses couldn't be far away, he reasoned. Unfortunately, he was wrong because, by the time of this writing, John had still not found his shades and the story has become something of a family joke. The punchline has it that the ghost is now wearing the missing glasses.

When John and his older brother went to bed one Christmas night, they left their new toys spread out in their grandmother's living room. During the night they heard one of their new toys running and, when they came down to the living room on Boxing Day, they found the toy broken. However, no one in the house had been up during the night.

The ghost would also turn photographs of family members around so that their faces were toward the wall and, like many, many ghosts, this one also enjoyed playing with electricity by turning light switches on and off.

Recently, one of John's brothers was staying at their grand-mother's house. He remarked that near the top of the staircase he'd thought that he'd seen a shadow that he was unable to account for. Of course, his grandmother was not surprised and readily accepted that such a sighting was possible. The two relayed the incident to John's step-grandfather when he came home from work later that day. When the older man scoffed and pronounced such imaginings as nonsense, all the lights in the house went out.

Perhaps that was the ghost's way of confirming its own existence.

A Hollywood-Like Haunt

The old haunted house near Appleton in the Ottawa Valley is all but invisible from the road. That's probably a good thing for the serenity of the owners, because there is no doubt this ghost story would make a terrific movie. Both the setting and the plot are right out of Hollywood.

When the place changed hands in the mid-1970s, the new owners were delighted, although mildly puzzled at its reasonable selling price. The price was so low that it almost seemed that the vendors were anxious to be rid of the property. The situation became even more intriguing when the purchasers discovered that they had gotten more for their money than had been initially evident: the property even included a small cemetery containing seven graves.

Investigation revealed that the house had been built in 1830 for a wealthy couple. It was a large home, and so the man building it invited his spinster sister to share the place with him and his wife. Their lives were the very embodiment of peace and quiet until the death of another brother left twelve children orphaned. Rather than have their nieces and nephews scattered throughout the countryside and raised by strangers, the couple and the spinster sister took the children in. The strain of raising the youngsters was too much for the sister and, by the time she died, she had gone very nearly insane. And, it seems, the tormented woman's spirit has never left the place.

At least now the new owners had an explanation for the strange visions they occasionally got out of the corners of their eyes. They also had a clear explanation for the entity's unwelcoming reaction to their daughter. The poor soul had suffered terribly in life because children had been brought into the home, and now here was another one disturbing her eternity.

Fortunately, the family adjusted quickly to life in their real estate bargain—even if it was a haunted house.

This Ghost Comes and Goes

Kathryn MacKay, publicist for the Thousand Islands Playhouse in Gananoque, seemed almost disappointed that the theatre was not home to a ghost. She wrote, "as far as I know, there is no history [of] spectres or ghouls at the Playhouse, [although] it is a very old building. It was a canoe club before it was a theatre, but it doesn't seem that anyone wants to haunt it."

As best good luck would have it, though, she soon made up for that initial disappointment. "[T]he house that many of the actors stay in while performing in Gananoque does seem to be inhabited by some sort of benevolent spectre."

It seems that the house in question was owned by a man who worked for the town's power plant.

The house where the actors playing at the Gananoque Playhouse stay is home to a ghost with a regular routine.

"Every spring, employees of the plant clean up around the falls and river that provide Gananoque with its power," Kathryn noted.

The former owner "failed to wear any safety equipment. [He] slipped and fell in[to the water] and drowned. It is his ghost that is assumed to be haunting the house. Supernatural phenomena around the house include lights going on and off without anyone near the switch, a ghostly presence felt on the stairs, in the kitchen dogs growl at unseen intruders, and footsteps are heard on the stairs."

Judging by the times these disturbances are heard and felt, it is reasonable to assume that the town worker is not yet aware that he's dead. For, just as he would have been in life, he's usually absent from the house during the day. Then he returns to "his" home at the end of each day and spends the nights there, possibly just going about the routine he enjoyed during his lifetime.

It's probably also reasonable to assume that the man was not a lover of live theatre or surely he would have accompanied at least one of the actors to the playhouse on occasion.

Sam Lived in Kitchener

Whenever I'm invited to present writing workshops to youngsters, I always base their writing assignment on one of my ghost stories. Occasionally after I've read a selection, students will volunteer a tale or two of their own. That is how I came to hear about a family in Kitchener and their haunted house. Because I was not able to contact the family directly, I have changed their name to "Leggasse."

Weekends for the Leggasse family were often spent camping. Before they left for their trips, Mrs. Leggasse always made a point of checking to make sure that all the lights in their house were turned off. Despite her diligence, the house lights were almost inevitably shining brightly upon the family's arrival home days later.

Looking for a logical explanation to an illogical event, Mr. Leggasse insisted that they must accidentally have left the lights in the house turned on. Unfortunately for his comforting theory, the incident was repeated many times, even on weekends when everyone knew that the house had been checked over carefully.

Many families name their ghosts, and the Leggasse family was no different. "Sam" became a part of the household. Perhaps this recognition gave the ghost strength because, one night, in the wee hours, he allowed himself to be seen by one of the Leggasse daughters. The girl had come home late, when the rest of the family was fast asleep. She'd gone directly to bed but had not been able to fall asleep because there were footsteps in the hallway outside her bedroom. In frustration, the youngster opened her bedroom door and, just for an instant, saw a dark image of a man. Moments later, the apparition vanished before her eyes.

Before the child could decide whether or not to tell anyone of the sighting, her sister summoned her to her own bedroom where she had quite a display to show off. Every picture on the walls of her room had been flipped over and was now hanging facing the wall.

The family seems to have outlasted the haunting, for my young informant assured me, "He isn't in their house any more," before adding the understated kicker, "but who knows."

Archie

In the early days of the twentieth century, Archibald Rosamond's textile mills near Almonte made him a wealthy man. When he built his home in 1918, Rosamond was well able to afford to indulge his every whim—and he did. The man thoroughly enjoyed living in the house until he died in 1945.

Judging from some of the experiences of more recent owners, Mr. Rosamond has continued to enjoy being in his house—even after his death.

They frequently smelled pipe smoke, although no one in the family smoked a pipe. They would find heavy pieces of furniture had moved, apparently on their own. Smaller objects would regularly go missing completely. Oddly, it was the sense of a slightly disapproving presence that was the most bothersome. This distinct feeling of not only being watched, but also of being somehow disparaged, was what drove the home-owners to begin making general inquiries of some of the older townsfolk.

It didn't take long for someone to figure out that Archibald Rosamond's spirit had remained behind in the home that he'd built. He not only smoked a pipe, but delighted in performing silly pranks. His former colleagues thought that pranks such as moving a piece of furniture just enough to be noticeable were quite typical of the man's behaviour.

They were also able to explain why certain areas of the house were more haunted than others. Those areas—the attic and the living room—were his favourites in life and had apparently remained his favourites in death.

Jane's Mirror

There is a strong correlation between ghosts and power sources. It seems safe to say that ethereal beings require—or are drawn to—things electric or electronic. Over the years I've heard many stories about electrical appliances malfunctioning in a house that's known to be haunted. Televisions will change channels by themselves, washing machines will turn on to the spin cycle when no one's been near them and so on. Dramatic support for this theory is that radio stations are frequently homes to ghosts.

For those reasons, I was not surprised that an important component of this next ghost story included a stove, an air conditioner and a washing machine all acting up in an apartment where apparitions had been spotted. I never did learn the young woman's name and know only that she was a university student when her ghostly experiences took place. For the sake of convenience, we shall call her "Jane."

Jane wondered whether a *faux pas* in interior decoration actually initiated all the trouble. As soon as she discovered that according to Feng Shui, the Oriental art of home-arranging, a mirror facing the foot of a bed brought bad luck, she dispensed with the mirror. Unfortunately, its removal seems to have been too late to prevent an all-out haunting.

The bedroom mirror played a significant role in all the sightings. The first apparition in the mirror to disturb Jane's serenity was an especially menacing one. It raised its arms in a gesture that the young woman took to be a threat. Its yellow eyes glowed menacingly. Its body seemed to be roughly the shape of a human's, but more fluid in composition.

The next time, not just one but two spectres invaded Jane's bedroom. Again the eyes were glowing, but this time they were red, not yellow. The spectres wore identical grey, hooded robes but were of very dissimilar heights. Something about their bearing indicated to Jane that these were evil creatures. Frighteningly, they merely stood still, their arms crossed in front of themselves, and stared at her.

By now Jane was beginning to suspect some connection between the mirror and the visions. Not wanting to give up the mirror, because it had useful properties during daylight hours, Jane merely moved it to an oblique angle. She felt assured with this new arrangement, as she could no longer see any reflection in the mirror while in her bed. Unfortunately, her feelings of assurance were misplaced. The next morning she beheld a holographic image of a woman suspended in the mirror.

The details of the image stayed with Jane and she described the vision's apparel in detail: a long, Victorian-looking gown with a high collar of frilly lace. Despite the raven-black hair, the woman's image was not an attractive manifestation, for her face was decomposing and partially skeletal. Seconds later the image was gone.

Jane saw one more apparition before putting the mirror away permanently. That last manifestation was a dreadful sight— a disembodied and decomposing head. That day she rearranged her bedroom furniture and put the mirror into storage. Unfortunately, that precaution was not sufficient to terminate the hauntings—it only changed them.

The next image to appear manifested itself in the spot where her bed had been when the seemingly possessed mirror was a part of the decor. This entity was the most persistent yet. For months it came and went of its own volition and on its own timetable. Its visits were so frequent that Jane was able to photograph the ghost. On film the image did not glow as it did when viewed with the naked eye, but instead presented a diffuse shadow.

Jane moved from the haunted apartment but kept in touch with other residents of the building. Through those connections she heard that the haunting had continued with the apartment's next occupants.

The Presence in the Portrait

Museums and archives are often haunted. The artifacts they house frequently arrive endowed with spiritual energy from their former abodes. Ted and Suzanne Currie of Gravenhurst are part-time antique dealers. They no longer run the store they once did, but Ted Currie well remembered opening up the shop in the morning and finding their merchandise was not how they had left when they'd locked the store the night before.

"Suzanne was a doll collector. When we'd come in in the morning seven out of ten [dolls] would have fallen over," Ted related.

Since they no longer operate an actual antique store but are still involved with the business, they often bring very old and very special articles into their home. Like curators of public repositories, they also, occasionally, inadvertently house stray energies that accompany these items. And that was exactly what happened when Ted purchased a small picture.

"I purchased a Victorian portrait of a young lady. We bought this at an auction," Ted began, before explaining that he remembered the specifics well. "We have a friend who was the auctioneer and I was so mad because I couldn't buy a thing. I was being blown out on everything."

Despite his disappointment, Ted knew that he'd have to keep his emotions in check. "When you're an antique dealer you've got to stick to that budget," he asserted. Keeping that in mind, while at the same time wanting to make an effort to relieve his frustration, he struck upon a compromise. He told himself he would not leave the auction that day empty-handed.

"There happened to be a pile of pictures. A bunch of old frames and it was toward the end of the sale and they went for something like $3. I bought them almost out of spite. In behind [one of the frames] there was a Victorian, hand-coloured picture of a little girl. It was a pretty big picture but it was pretty badly worn. I thought, at least I've come back with something."

Little did Ted Currie know how prophetic that thought would turn out to be. His wife took one look at it and pronounced, "I don't like that picture."

Suzanne's reasons for her negative feelings were quite specific. She told Ted, "She's a very unhappy little girl. Very unhappy."

Although the Curries did not give the little girl a name, it is interesting that they never referred to the picture as that—a picture—but rather by feminine pronouns. For example, Ted explained, "She refused to hang straight. She's had three major falls where on two occasions she missed…a…jug-and-bowl set [worth about $400]."

The picture doesn't have that effect just on the Curries either. "Everywhere she's been everybody will say, 'I don't like her,'" he explained.

The fact that those who saw it were not taken by the portrait probably isn't surprising. Currie describes the image in the frame as "having a frown. It was a photo that was colour-enhanced so they [the subjects of the photos] had to have these metal clamps around their necks for the long exposures. It's very hard to hold a smile so what happened was it came off as a very melancholy portrait."

"She" did not stay up on the hooks the Curries tried to suspend "her" from for any length of time and, even when she did hang on the wall, she was, despite their care in placing the supports, always at an angle. The sad photograph had a strange effect on objects around it as well.

"We'd have books pop off shelves. It was just a terrific amount of trouble with this girl but for some reason everybody kind of got used to her," Ted Currie acknowledged.

In order to help decorate the stage and set the scene for a play the local theatre company was producing, the Curries lent out the strange portrait.

"It was a Victorian England thriller. The set was a beautiful English Victorian parlour with a hallway and one of the pictures they borrowed from me was this little girl. I never said anything to them at the time but I thought it'll be interesting to hear back whether she ever hung straight. The night before we went to see [the show] they had a great event. During the final bow one gentleman [an actor] suffered a heart attack. It wasn't fatal but he was pretty sick. They had to get a substitute. They brought him [the new actor] up and he actually used the script in his hand. He was such a good actor that it didn't matter. You forgot that he was carrying a book around....We were sitting in the front row and when the hall door opened into the parlour... it was the most amazing thing. People kind of gasped...here's the picture of the little girl—she's as askew as she could possibly get without falling off," Ted recalled.

When the play's run was over, Ted went to pick up the period pieces that he had lent to the theatre company as props. He inquired at the time as to whether there'd been any problems with any of the set decorations. He mentioned that during the performance, which he and his wife had enjoyed, they'd noticed that one picture had been hanging on the wall at a strange angle.

The theatre representative responded, "You know, we tried everything with that picture to get it hanging properly but no way, so we just got to the point where we figured it must be the vibrations on the floor."

Ted did not dispute the conclusion that the theatre cast had come to. After all, they hadn't asked for his opinion on the possible causes.

And where's the seemingly possessed portrait now?

"She's hanging in our family room," Ted said. "I've been offered enormous amounts of money for her but that's not the point. The point is this little girl had three major falls off the wall, [yet she] never cracked, and [she] missed the $400 jug-and-bowl set. Wherever this portrait hung it would always attract attention."

Lives Disrupted by Poltergeist

There is no denying that certain places are haunted—they are simply home to ghosts. The old bank building that currently houses Canada's Hockey Hall of Fame is an excellent example of a place being haunted. However, poltergeists are a type of ghost that is always associated with a person—not a place. Poltergeists are also known for the chaos that they create. They are noisy, active spirits.

A classic example of a poltergeist presence existed in the affluent Forest Hill area of Toronto. It is, I think, unfortunate that the tale has been recorded strictly from the perspective of the families whose homes were visited by the destructive entity, and not at all from the viewpoint of the suffering youngster who was clearly the vehicle for the poltergeist's activities.

Many households in the affected area employed a full complement of domestic staff. Others, such as the Sherman, the Donnenfeld and the Young households, were not such complex operations and required domestic help only on a part-time basis. These three families all lived within a few blocks of one another and, as a result, arranged to share one young woman's services as a domestic servant.

The plan might have worked well except that, along with the maid, they also unwittingly welcomed her poltergeist into their homes. The Sherman home was the first to become aware that something was very wrong. The family listened in terror as heart-wrenching moans emanated from an unidentifiable source and knocking and whistling sounds echoed through their house.

Understandably shaken by the frightening and mysterious sounds, the Shermans were completely unprepared for what was to come next—explosions that left huge, gaping holes in the plaster walls of their large, luxurious home. Mrs. Sherman knew that she'd endured enough when a big chunk of plaster fell from the ceiling of her baby's room into his crib—only minutes after she'd lifted the child out of the bed.

Thinking that the house itself was the cause of the problem, Mrs. Sherman sent the maid (and her poltergeist) to the nearby Donnenfeld home, and she packed sufficient clothes for herself and her baby and sought shelter elsewhere. Although they didn't realize it at the time, the Shermans were left with a badly damaged but completely calm house.

Not surprisingly, the supernatural sounds started up now in the Donnenfeld home. The disturbances that had struck such terror in the Sherman family's hearts were now at work in Mrs. Donnenfeld's home. The connection between the apparent possession and the young servant's presence was beginning to be noted. But Mrs. Donnenfeld had been seriously ill and was therefore not nearly as well equipped to deal with the haunting as expeditiously as the Shermans. More importantly, she was in need of the help the young girl presumably could provide. However, after enduring only a few days of unnatural activity in her house, Mrs. Donnenfeld knew something had to be done.

She began by calling in the Toronto police. Not surprisingly, the force was unable to offer any solution to her problem. In desperation, Mrs. Donnenfeld decided that she would try to cope on her own: she sent the maid to the Youngs.

Duplicating the newly appreciated calm in the Sherman house, the Donnenfeld home also became quiet once again—and the ghostly ruckus began anew at the Young family's residence. By now the pattern was clear. But, rather than trying to find some way of exorcising the presence that was accompanying the young woman, each affected family responded completely selfishly by merely sending her away.

There is no record as to whether there was ever a resolution to this chronicle of poltergeist possession.

Sisters Stayed On

Making a commercial recording would be a nerve-wracking experience anywhere, but during the 1970s in a particular recording studio in Toronto, the process could have been even more stress-inducing: the place was haunted.

When well-known composer Ben McPeek bought the old house on Hazelton, he had no idea that it was haunted. By the time the place was renovated in 1982, he, his sons and many of their clients had seen the apparition of an old woman. Research into the background of the haunted house revealed that two sisters had lived together in the three-storey home while waiting for their husbands to return from the war. At least one of the women continued her patient vigil long after her death, for she was frequently seen wandering both the second floor and the attic areas of the house. People who saw her reported that the spectre often stopped at a window, perhaps checking to see if her beloved might be walking toward the house. A woman who worked at the recording studio once refused to enter the empty building until some of her co-workers had arrived because, as she approached the house, she spotted the image of a woman at an attic window.

Occasionally the ghost could also be something of a nuisance, rearranging articles about the house and making her voice heard even when her image couldn't be seen.

One night the occupants were driven from the house when an unseen presence began knocking record albums off the shelves and making scratching sounds at the door to the room they were in. When they opened the door to see who or what was making the sounds, there was no one there.

Ghosts frequently react to renovations done to "their" building. Often their ghostly activities increase. In this case, however, after the owner did extensive renovations to the place, the ghostly goings-on ceased completely. Perhaps the deceased woman felt that the changes to the place rendered it no longer appealing for her habitation.

A Well-Haunted Farm

Scott Wing is now a firefighter living in Canmore, Alberta, but he will never forget his visits to a haunted farmhouse north of Whitby, Ontario.

He was staying with a friend who was renting a room in the 150-year-old house. At the time of its construction, the place, of course, had not been wired for electricity. By the time Scott's friend moved in, however, power had been added, but the electrical panel was located outside the house, braced up on a post in the yard.

It would seem that the entity that haunted the rambling old two-storey rural residence was probably from a simpler, non-electrical era, for he or she certainly liked to tinker with the power.

"Being an old farmhouse," Scott recalled, "the power would quite often click off."

Despite this obvious deficiency in wiring, the occupants had a full selection of electrical appliances. There was even a "light box" with miniature coloured lights on a black background, which when connected to the speakers, showed "different light patterns when you turned the music on."

Because the circuit breakers were occasionally overloaded and not convenient to get at, "you wouldn't exactly jump up every time the power went off," Scott explained.

Besides, you really didn't have to get up if all you wanted was visual entertainment, because "whenever the [landlady] was talking and the power was off, the light box would light up."

A barn, roughly dating to the same era as the house and now also wired for electricity, stood on the property. The farm family kept chickens and horses in the front part of the barn and they, along with Scott's friend, kept their dogs at the far end of the barn.

"It was your typical 150-year-old barn," Scott related. "It was huge."

One night, long after sunset, Scott and his friend went out to the barn to give the dogs their evening meal.

"It's pitch black outside and all of a sudden the lights [in the barn] went out. We figured one of the horses had bumped the [light] switch over by the front door or again, the circuit breaker [was to blame for the power outage]," Scott said. "We made our way back out past the chickens and horses. The switch was fine, so okay, the circuit breaker must [have been tripped], but no, it's still on too."

It took the two men several minutes to figure out what had caused the sudden blackout in the barn.

"The light bulbs above the horses and above the chickens had both been unscrewed. How did that happen?" he asked rhetorically. "The roof was probably twelve feet high. You couldn't touch the roof. You'd have needed a ladder and there wasn't any noise at all. I have to admit that was definitely on the weird side."

When they related the incident to the resident landlady, she was not surprised. She'd actually seen the mischievous ghost on occasion.

"She told us she'd turned around one day and she saw an image of a little boy. The little boy said, 'your cat's sick.'"

Then, as quickly as it had appeared, the vision vanished. Not knowing what else to do, the woman "picked up the cat and took it to the vet. The cat had some kind of a heart murmur and if it hadn't been addressed it would have died," Scott reported.

After that incident, the lady of the house was understandably curious about the presence in her home.

"She started [wondering] who is this little kid floating inside my house," Scott recalled. "As it turned out, the kid had died of pneumonia about 150 years ago when the house was first built. To him it was still 'his house.'"

The room Scott's friend was renting might originally have belonged to the little waif, for no matter how warm the rest of the house was, his room was consistently cold.

"It was freezing. There was frost on the windows [but] when you walked out of that room it was warm. Walk back in and it's freezing," Scott said. He concluded his story about that house with, "There was no question about it. Something was definitely going 'bump' in the night."

Cranky Mr. Legge

Some ghosts simply can't get enough attention. Even when Mr. Legge's Ice Cream Parlour and Dessert Cafe, housed in the late Frank Legge's former home, Oak Manor, was named after him, his ghost could still, occasionally, be a nuisance. However, the once well-haunted building no longer offers ice cream for sale but now houses Oak Manor Estate Wines, and it may no longer be haunted.

Legend has it that the late Mr. Legge, the original owner of the *circa* 1920s house, was a decidedly unpleasant character with an inclination to overindulge in spirits. He must have been deeply attached to Oak Manor, because he and other members of his family have stayed with it for many years after their deaths.

The staff of a recording company that once occupied the old two-and-one-half-storey house came to refer to the place as "Joke Manor" instead of "Oak Manor." An enumeration of the many ghostly pranks the staff endured explains why the nickname was indeed most appropriate.

Pictures on the walls would be found upside down when no one had been near them. Drawers in filing cabinets would open and close independently, phantom footsteps could be heard from a vacant area of the house and the smell of cigar smoke frequently wafted through the place. Fortunately, for the most part, the employees accepted their invisible interloper with good grace—his presence wasn't a factor in their decision to relocate.

An antique shop occupied the premises for most of the 1980s, and the proprietor lived in the house next door. This proximity not only made her commute appealing but it also gave her the opportunity to watch the lights in Oak Manor go on and off at night when the place was supposed to be empty. The sounds of footsteps were frequently heard coming from parts of the house the shop's owner knew were empty at the time.

Despite her skeptical nature, the proprietor was highly suspicious that she was sharing her space with at least one ghost. Her first step was to check county records on the historically significant house. Through the official records, the business owner discovered that one of the Legges' children, Homer, had died in 1977 after being estranged from the family for years.

Next, the antique expert called in a psychic. What was revealed in that investigation explained a great deal. Homer's estrangement from the family apparently continued even after death. The psychic inferred that, although a small marker indicates that he is buried beside his family, his body does not really lie there. This fact, the psychic felt, contributed to his soul's unrest. In addition, she detected two deaths associated with the house, and one was an especially violent murder. Someone had been killed by being pushed down the staircase.

The other death was that of an infant who had been stillborn. That information explained a great deal to the woman. Two of the items for sale in the shop were cribs. One night, when she locked up the shop, the small beds were set up as if ready for a baby, but the next morning they were all in pieces.

And then there was the frightening incident when the antique shop owner and a customer were standing in the second-storey hall. They were discussing the death of a child, and in the middle of their conversation a picture came off the wall and flew across the room. Although these ghostly activities frightened the woman, she now suspects that the ghost was actually fond of her. She had decided to move on to other endeavours and, when it came time to leave the building for the last time, she could not get the door to open. It wasn't locked and it had never given her any trouble before, but she simply could not budge it and, as a result, was effectively held captive in the Legges' former home for some time.

The next occupants were Danny and Debbie McLellan, who took over the building to house the ice cream parlour they planned to open. Perhaps they thought they'd win the ghost over right from the beginning by naming their business in his honour. The old place had been vacant for a time and was in need of renovations before they could open Mr. Legge's Ice Cream Parlour. Toward this end, they hired workers to redo the place to suit their needs. Two of those workers didn't last long on the job. They fled the place vowing never to return, after witnessing the image of a man running across the loft area of the house only to vanish into a wall.

Danny McLellan had always considered himself a skeptic. Even so, he could not deny that there were a number of unexplained occurrences in and around the old place. Many of those events were the sorts of things anyone who's used to being in a haunted building will quickly credit to a ghostly presence. Phantom footsteps and unexplainable whistling were frequently heard. McLellan also learned to associate the distinctive aroma of cigar smoke with the arrival of at least one of the building's ghostly presences.

There was a grand piano stored on the premises. For years it had not been cared for, it was never played and it was badly out of tune. Despite all this, it would occasionally sound a chord when no one was near it.

While the ice cream shop was downstairs, the McLellans rented out the second floor of the building as an apartment. Their tenants frequently got more than they bargained for. In addition to the cigar smoke and sounds of footsteps, the renters spoke of hearing furniture being moved, keys being rattled and unidentifiable banging noises. Occasionally the disturbances were severe enough to keep them awake. They discovered, however, that yelling at the presence to be quiet was usually an effective antidote.

One night they actually saw an apparition of an old lady sitting in a wheelchair. Later they were able to confirm, through archival photos, that the image they saw was that of Edith Legge, Mr. Legge's wife.

The current owners of the Legges' former home don't feel that the place is haunted and, by now, they may be absolutely accurate. Perhaps all the Legges are finally at rest.

Chapter

THE
HAUNTED
STAGE

A Double-Decker Haunt

From conception to renovation, there has never been anything ordinary about the theatre at 189 Yonge Street, Toronto.

On December 15, 1913, amid dignitaries, pageantry and hoopla, the enormous "Loew's Yonge Street Theatre" opened. Two months later, with considerably less fanfare, the upper theatre, the Winter Garden, opened. It seated 1410 patrons (compared to the lower theatre's capacity of 2149) and therefore could hardly be called intimate, but both halls were luxurious—to the point of pretension. It was the perfect home for vaudeville.

The double-decker playhouse was popular with Toronto's theatre-going public—but the good times were destined to be short lived. Vaudeville was a dying art and, what was worse, some young upstarts were promoting moving pictures with sound—the actual voices of the actors. Difficult as it was for those in the business to imagine, these newfangled talking pictures were steadily gaining in popularity.

Eventually Loew had to acknowledge the obvious and, to retain any hope at all of remaining viable, he installed speakers in the larger, lower theatre and began to show "talkies," along with every other cinema in the world. He never did update the Winter Garden Theatre and the doors of the once-glamorous second-storey auditorium were locked in 1928. The place remained virtually sealed for more than a half-century.

World events raced over and around the entombed Winter Garden Theatre. Less than a year and a half after the upper theatre closed, the New York stock market crashed, signalling the beginning of the Great Depression. The tragic chaos that was World War II began and ended. Families moved en masse to the suburbs, forever changing the fabric of our society. A man walked on the moon. The fashion conscious decked themselves in polyester bell-bottoms and love beads. Then the computer began to make the same kinds of strides into modern lives that the motorcar had when vaudeville was king.

The passing of the years brought changes to the lower theatre. Until the 1960s, it was a popular venue for the movie-going public. But the advent of suburbia and television shifted the demographics, and "Loew's," as it was now commonly called, could no longer attract the crowds required to fill the huge hall. With this loss of patronage came an equal loss of revenue, and the theatre could no longer afford to run the top-rated movies. Consequently, management began to show the types of films that they could afford to rent and, in short order, Loew's became a theatre avoided by respectable audiences.

Demolition appeared to be a financial inevitability for the double-decker hall—until December 1, 1981, when the Ontario Heritage Foundation bought the building. The far-sighted historians saw the importance of preserving and restoring the place, not only as an excellent example of an early-twentieth-century entertainment venue, but also as a pair of functioning and revenue-generating theatres.

When the Heritage Foundation workers reopened the upper theatre to begin the enormous renovation project, they walked into an eerie, though unintended, time-capsule. The cavernous old hall stood as it had after the final performance in 1928. Here, the impossible had happened—time had stood still. Original vaudeville scenery remained where it was last used more than fifty years before. Performers' notes were found pinned to walls in dressing rooms. Old ticket stubs lay where they'd been dropped by patrons, many of whom were no doubt long since deceased. The surreal surroundings, disrupted only by the occasional pigeon fluttering about, appeared to be about as empty and lifeless as a place could be.

Once renovations got under way, however, the Winter Garden Theatre suddenly didn't seem to be empty at all. Right from the beginning, groups of energetic and enthusiastic volunteer workers began to note "strange goings on," according to Alison Truelove of the Ontario Heritage Foundation.

On more than one occasion, as the workers stood and watched, a row of spring-loaded seats would fold down as though a group of people had just seated themselves to watch a show. The seat bottoms would remain down for a time and then, in unison, would fold up against the chair backs again as though those same unseen people had risen and left their seats after enjoying a performance.

Their curiosity understandably piqued, one group of volunteers took a Ouija board up to the theatre. Their initiative was rewarded immediately, as "Samuel" identified himself to them. Through the board, Samuel explained that he had been a trombone player in a Winter Garden vaudeville production in 1918. Presumably he'd enjoyed his tenure at the then-fashionable hall and had returned to it in death, hoping to spend a peaceful eternity surrounded by the theatre's silent splendour.

Because so many of the volunteers had witnessed the strange phenomenon of a row of seats folding down for no apparent reason, they were convinced that, as personable as Samuel might be, he was not the only presence in the place. They asked the spirit of the trombone player if he was alone or if there were, indeed, other spirits in the hall.

Yes, there were others, many others, confirmed Samuel. "May we speak with some of them?" the curious group probed. "No" came Samuel's unarguable response. It seemed the long-dead musician was enjoying once again being in the limelight, for he steadfastly refused to let the people communicate with any of the other spirits in the building.

Although no one's been able to "talk" to any of the other ghosts of the Winter Garden, those silent spirits have managed to make their presence known just the same.

"There are three elevators in the building," Alison Truelove explained. "They are all hand operated from the inside, so technically they cannot go anywhere unless someone is in them. Despite this, after one elevator is used it doesn't stay at that floor but always returns to a particular floor."

As well, theatre patrons have reported seeing a woman dressed in Edwardian clothing in the lobby. She appears only fleetingly and, by the time the person seeing her realizes that what he or she is seeing is highly irregular and either looks again or tries to draw a companion's attention to the unusual image, it is gone.

Neither Samuel nor any of his supernatural colleagues have ever been threatening at all. They usually seem to merely exist, refreshingly unaware of time as we perceive it, although Alison credits one of the spirits in the Winter Garden Theatre with preventing her from having a serious accident. She's never seen anything in either of the two theatres to indicate that they're haunted but she has "felt something."

"I was alone in the theatre doing inventory," she explained. The objects the woman needed to assess next were in a locked room. Her mind only on the job at hand, Alison unlocked the door. "But something made me not open it."

She had never been into that particular area before and later found out that she probably would not have been able to find the light switch. In searching for it, Alison might not have noticed an open door in the unexplored room. That open door led to a potentially lethal sheer drop. Alison's sudden, strange and strong conviction not to enter the room may well have saved her life.

The Winter Garden Theatre, where Sam and his friends are hauntingly present.

Alison's not sure where her abrupt change in plan came from, although she does seem to feel that the idea didn't originate in her own mind. She's understandably grateful, however, to whoever or whatever put it there.

Since its reopening, the revived theatre played a prominent role in the movie *Camilla*, the legendary Jessica Tandy's last film. And it has been host to a number of spectacularly successful shows. Andrew Lloyd Weber's *Cats* enjoyed two sold-out years and the rock opera *Tommy* wowed thousands of theatre-goers. Patrons were consistently as impressed with their surroundings as they were with the performances they came to see.

And so, at the Winter Garden Theatre in Toronto, Canada, the living and the dead now coexist in peace. The many spirits that inhabit the place may even appreciate all the time and trouble that has gone into reviving their once-again glorious home. Perhaps one of those spirits is the ghost of the theatre's original creator, Marcus Loew, now able to enjoy his crowning corporate accomplishment into eternity.

Grand Ghosts

The history of the Grand Theatre in London virtually demands that it be haunted. And it is.

Theatre magnate Ambrose Small was proud of each of the theatres that he owned, but this one, built around the year 1900 on Richmond Street, was his absolute favourite. It is not surprising that, even though Ambrose Small mysteriously vanished from downtown Toronto in December 1919, his spirit has chosen to inhabit this beautiful old building in London from that day forward.

The first sighting in the London theatre may have been shortly after Small was last seen alive. The night watchman swore that he had talked to the owner that night, although there is no record of Small intending to leave his home town of Toronto that night. The employee's claim was taken seriously enough that the entire building was searched—in vain.

Former Grand manager and confirmed skeptic Paul Eck remembers looking into the balcony area of the theatre and seeing a "distinct shadow" for which he could find no cause. When he worked alone late at night in the theatre, it wasn't tiredness or workload that would occasionally send him home earlier than he'd planned. It was the stress of knowing that he was inside a locked, supposedly empty building and yet hearing phantom footsteps on stairways and seeing lights turn off by themselves.

On the night that actress Charmion King was the last to leave the building, she stood, momentarily frozen in awe, as a strange and apparently sourceless light "walked" along an elevated catwalk.

But Ambrose Small's ghost is not the only one in the theatre. An apparition of a woman, believed to be that of a former cleaning woman, has been reported on the theatre's stairs. And when the Grand hosted a production of the James Reaney play about the Black Donnellys of nearby Lucan, the entire clan— or their manifestations anyway—left their usual haunt (now Robert Salts' property; see "The Donnellys Are Here," p. 107) and joined the cast and crew in London.

It is Ambrose, however, who is considered the theatre's resident spook and everyone associated with the Grand greatly appreciates his presence there, for Small's ghost is commonly credited with having saved the theatre from unintended demolition.

Immediately following its 1976–77 season, the theatre closed its doors for what everyone knew was going to be a major renovation. The old place was showing every day of its age. The roof leaked, the floors creaked, it was often cold in the winter and warm in the summer—this building was clearly down on its heels. It needed to be renovated and that's exactly what was planned.

The reconstruction project was not merely an engineering and architectural feat; it was, in equal part, a work of art. Before the crews could begin rebuilding, they had to take down the deteriorating old walls. Thus it came to pass that every wall in the place had been dismantled, except for the west wall of the building, which included the enormous proscenium arch. This arch, with its irreplaceable hand-painted mural, had always been the theatre's focal point.

Suddenly and inexplicably, the backhoe working on the west wall ceased to function. Some people say that the machine stalled and wouldn't restart. Others that the operator responded to a hunch and simply turned the engine off. Whatever the cause, the result was that Ambrose's beloved proscenium arch was saved. When engineers investigated at the place where the backhoe had stopped, they found that the machine had stopped one brick short of removing the last support preventing this priceless architectural feature from crashing to the ground! Workers and Grand Theatre employees generally credit the protective spirit of Ambrose Small for averting an inevitable disaster. The wall was immediately shored up, and today the single brick that for moments held the arch safe from ruin is on display in a showcase in the Grand Theatre.

Another reason for the former owner's spirit to have a particular interest in the west wall came out during a seance, held some time later in the darkened theatre. During the seance, a spirit voice counselled that "the secret to Ambrose's death lives in the west wall."

Despite his inherent interest in preserving the Grand, Ambrose's presence can be something of a nuisance. He has appeared in actors' dressing rooms and caused problems during performances. During the run of *Anne of Green Gables*, Small's ghost was blamed for the sounds of phantom footsteps that were heard in the balcony, as well as the sand that mysteriously poured from the fly floor during a rehearsal.

More recently, his image was spotted by an actress while she was on stage. The sight of an apparition floating in a reclining position and as though suspended above the heads of the unsuspecting audience must have given the woman's stage composure a jolt.

In typically ghost-like fashion, Ambrose's spirit has caused electrical appliances to act in peculiar manners. During the last season before the massive renovations got under way, a camera malfunctioned and, for reasons no one was ever able to identify, ruined the film that had been loaded into it. More recently, a hissing sound for which no source could ever be found vibrated throughout the "haunted house."

The proscenium arch in the Grand Theatre was saved from accidental destruction by a mysterious, unseen force.

Ambrose is also presumed to have been the person who opened the production booth door and peered in while a play was in progress. As soon as the producer acknowledged the face, it disappeared. She later described the ghost as having a white face with dark hair and a beard that left the area around the eyes white—a description that, according to old photos, could easily have applied to Ambrose.

There is no record of Small having had a particularly robust sense of humour during his life, but he may have been responsible for a practical joke years after his death. Three bats mysteriously appeared during the Grand's production of *Dracula*. If it was indeed the ghost of Ambrose Small that caused the flying rodents to suddenly appear, then it's obvious that the man's theatrical skills had not diminished, even after death.

The Phantom of the Opera House

The building has been a landmark for nearly a century, but there is little about today's Gravenhurst Opera House and Arts Centre that is recognizable from the floundering theatre it was just a few years ago. Even the name has undergone renovation and the restored old place is now commonly called "The Op."

Thanks to a huge expenditure of time, money and effort, the theatre is once again as splendid as it originally was. And, happily, it seems to have remained haunted.

The spirit at The Op is thought to be that of Ben, a former lighting technician who fell to his death while working in the theatre. Ben's presence is generally cited when doors slam close unexpectedly or a draft or a spot of cold manifests itself in an otherwise warm area. Like many ghosts, Ben likes to tinker with things electrical and has been known to turn light switches on and off when no one else is near them.

The theatre depends heavily on volunteers to keep The Op operational. One of those volunteers, Lee Madden, reported to Martha Anderson of *The Muskokan* that she has heard phantom footsteps, which were then followed by the sound of a door closing heavily. Lee also spoke of a considerably closer encounter than that. She suspects that the ghost laid its hand on her shoulder. Taking the tactile connection with the supernatural presence amazingly calmly, Lee merely informed the ghost that she was very busy and therefore needed to be left alone to continue her work. The spirit apparently obliged.

Considering that renovations often either provoke resident ghosts into further activity or, conversely, into leaving a place, it's reassuring to realize that the more things change at the Gravenhurst Opera House, the more they also seem to be remaining the same.

His Spirit Remained

The late 1940s was an exciting time for Ontarians. The province was alive with activity of all sorts. The economy was booming and the population was growing. Most importantly, the mood was optimistic—life, everyone was sure, would just keep getting better and better from now on.

New buildings shot up, seemingly overnight. The numbers of entertainment venues multiplied. Families torn apart by the war were now reunited and anxious to enjoy the fruits of their hard-won peace and newly acquired wealth. Attendance at the movies was reaching an all-time high. In order to capitalize on this trend, entrepreneurs built new movie houses in residential areas, knowing that they would recoup their investments with ticket sales.

One such cinema, known initially as the Vaughan, was built in 1947 in what was then Toronto's west end. Fifteen years before, there had been a funeral home at almost exactly that spot. But the owners were sure that, once the theatre was erected, the location would be associated with entertainment, not death. It was not to be: a suicide became the premier event at the new Vaughan Cinema.

On opening night a man rigged one of the weighted ropes for the theatre's curtain into a noose. Balancing his body weight against that of the sandbag intended to hold the curtain in place, he hanged himself. That suicide guaranteed that the theatre was a haunted house right from the beginning. The man's image was seen by patrons and staff alike over the building's forty-year history.

The spectre of the man so unhappy with his life that he chose to end it prematurely was likely not lonely during his long residency in the theatre, because the building was also haunted by the ghost of a woman. As her image appeared to be dressed in fashions that just predated the construction of the Vaughan Cinema, it was presumed that her presence was originally tied in with the former funeral home.

Over the years, the theatre changed names, changed focus and changed ownership, but the ghosts were constant presences until the building was demolished in the 1980s. Hopefully by now the restless spirits have moved on to their final resting place.

Ghosts Galore

In Toronto in 1907, the term "millionaire" really meant something—something considerably more than it does today, when houses routinely sell for that amount. Cawthra Mulock was one of those people who knew, from personal experience, exactly the implications of the word "millionaire," for the young man had attained that financial status himself. Because of this wealth, he was able to indulge virtually any wish that he might have had, and one of those was to construct a grand theatre for his home town. The Royal Alexandra Theatre, which *Showbusiness* magazine once referred to as "the most beautiful theatre on the North American continent," is the result of Mulock's lavish dream.

The Royal Alex's stage has hosted the best entertainers and entertainment the world has known. From 1913 until the early 1940s, the legendary Al Jolson occasionally performed there. Decades later, in 1997, the Alex put on the show *Jolson*, a tribute to the entertainer's life. During the entire run, the cast saw an eerie blue light floating above one of the balconies. One actor may have caught a glimpse of the long-dead performer when, as part of his role during a scene, he opened the hatch leading to the orchestra pit. There, dressed in old-fashioned clothing, sat the spectre of a man. Moments after he saw it, the image vanished and the unnerved actor had to continue his role as best he could, pretending that nothing extraordinary had happened.

That apparition, possibly Jolson himself, is one of many ghosts in the well-haunted Royal Alex. The existence of these spectres is so accepted that, when recently asked whether the theatre was haunted, Randy Alldread, publicity and promotions spokesman for the business, replied by forwarding a copy of an extensive article on the subject from a recent edition of the usually staid *Globe and Mail*.

Not surprisingly for a venue that has welcomed as many people through its doors as the Alex has, there have been numerous deaths both in the building and connected with the theatre. These deaths might partially account for its current gaggle of ghosts.

One of the presences remaining in the theatre is believed to be the spirit of a "flyman." (This term describes the person responsible for moving the equipment and scenery using a complex series of ropes strung from the stage up to the fly gallery.) On Halloween, 1994, Darrin Carter, the lighting man for the show *Crazy For You*, admitted seeing a headless spectre walk past him at his isolated post far above the stage. The sighting was so distinct that he was able to describe the apparition's clothes. Even if the ghost had appeared whole, with its head intact, Carter would still have known that what he had seen was not a flesh-and-blood human being. The area where he saw the image was completely isolated and he had a clear view of the only door leading to or from it—if a live person had opened that door and come through it, he would have known about it.

The flyman could not be lonely in his hereafter, for there are many spirits in the Alex to keep him company. Many people claim that they can still feel the presence of the theatre patron who died in her second-balcony seat while enjoying a production at the theatre.

The Royal Alexandra Theatre.

Employee Luis Rebelo is occasionally required to be alone in the Royal Alex overnight. The ghost stories surrounding the grand old dame of King Street West never fazed the man, for he was a determined skeptic. And he kept that attitude until his first encounter with the ghosts in the theatre. Coincidentally, that experience occurred as he worked his first-ever graveyard shift just after he had checked the building thoroughly and knew it to be empty.

Initially Rebelo heard sounds of conversations coming from the dressing-room area of the supposedly empty building. Wanting to know which of the actors had remained, he decided to phone through to each of the dressing-room extensions until he got an answer. Not one of Luis Rebelo's calls was answered, and yet he continued to hear the sorts of voice sounds that one associates with being at a party. He was even able to pick out a bit of what was being said, including the phrase, "Yes, yes, we'll have to do this again."

Hoping to catch at least a sign of the invisible intruders, Luis sprinkled powder on the floor outside the dressing-rooms and then left the area. Later, when he heard doors that he knew he had locked swinging open, he went to investigate more thoroughly. There were footsteps through the powder he'd spread.

Since his first encounters with the phantom voices, similar experiences have been frequent enough that Rebelo now accepts the ghosts' presence. He even thinks that another entity may have just been added to the roster. Rebelo worked closely with a man named Vic Egglestone. The two had devised a code, a rhythm on the door buzzer, to alert each other of who was wanting to come in.

Egglestone recently died after a long illness. Luis Rebelo is sure that the man's spirit remains in the theatre because not only has he heard the buzzer sound their distinctive and secret pattern but, when Rebelo responded, there was no one there.

The chair in the office that once belonged to Egglestone is a most ordinary chair, even though it occasionally acts in a most extraordinary way. Once when Rebelo entered the office, he saw the chair in the middle of the room. He attempted to move it to the side, but the small, standard-issue steno chair refused to budge. No matter how hard Luis Rebelo pushed it, he could not make Egglestone's old chair move.

Rebelo could not have been entirely surprised by this strange situation, for he has often sensed his former co-worker's presence in that small office. Occasionally, when he goes into the deceased man's office, it will have that extraordinary chill to it that has come to be associated with the presence of a ghost.

And so, the collection of ghosts at the theatre that Cawthra Mulock built shows no signs of decreasing.

An Attempted Introduction

In the late 1980s, employees at Toronto's Theatre Centre often had to work under rather trying circumstances. Almost from the moment the company moved into the nearly one-hundred-year-old premises, it was clear that the building was well and truly haunted.

Actors and production crew heard "something" walking around empty and locked parts of the building. The sounds of those phantom footsteps were frequently followed by doors slamming. Sometimes they heard the sounds of conversations seemingly coming from nowhere.

Most annoying of all, however, were the noisy spirit's pranks. Occasionally, when the employees needed a specific prop—a prop that they knew to be located in a particular place—they would find that it had disappeared.

Although all of those ghostly activities were undeniably unnerving, they were nothing compared to the time that the ghost perhaps tried to introduce himself to his new co-workers. One evening, the last person to leave had locked the building as always but, despite the overnight security, the next morning when the staff entered their offices, they discovered that "someone" had left an old funeral notice on one of their desks. Presumably the spirit was hoping to formally introduce himself to his more corporeal counterparts.

Chapter

RELATIVES RETURN

Ouija Board Experiences

The year was 1965. Al and Barb were young parents living in a small apartment building on Lawrence Avenue West in Toronto. Through their comings and goings they became acquainted with a few of their neighbours. Something of a friendship began to form with one particular family that lived on the second floor of the building—the Davies. After a few weeks of exchanging pleasantries in the corridors, it was proposed that the two couples get together for an evening.

Janet and Dick Davies asked if they could host the evening at their apartment. Their two children were at ages that made a disruption at bedtime difficult, whereas Al and Barb's daughter was young enough to be put to bed for the night in her carriage, which could be taken along wherever they chose to go.

Not one of the people interviewed for this retelling was able to recall how the evening's conversation wound itself around to the phenomenon of the Ouija board. In fact, none can remember having a particular interest in exploring the paranormal, which makes the evening's experience somewhat more of a supernatural puzzle. Evidently the topic did arise because, by the time midnight approached, the four young people had fashioned a home-made Ouija board using squares of paper on which they wrote the letters of the alphabet, numbers from zero to nine and the words "yes" and "no." These they spread out over the Davies dining-room table.

Janet volunteered the use of a delicate bone-china teacup as the planchette for the makeshift Ouija board. They turned off all the lights, added the requisite ambiance created by a lighted candle, seated themselves around the table and the impromptu seance began.

All the participants were excited at the prospect of dabbling in something new and unknown. In their naïveté they were extremely surprised when the teacup began to move around the table, pointing to letters and spelling out answers to the questions that they posed. Amid giggles of delight at their newly discovered powers, the four stayed hunched around the table, their fingertips resting lightly on the teacup, for well over an hour.

At about that point, for a long-forgotten reason, they decided to take a break. Whether the board "went cold" (stopped moving in response to queries) or whether one or more of the people involved simply wanted to stop for a while, cannot be recalled. After a short time away from the table, they all felt pulled back to the "game."

As soon as they got back to the table and put their fingers on the teacup-turned-planchette, it began to move, although no one had asked any questions. Startled, Dick, who'd become the spokesman for the little group, asked that the spirit moving the cup identify itself. It did so immediately, and the answer jolted Dick's composure. Apparently, they had somehow disturbed the spirit of Dick's deceased father.

Dick had been the older man's namesake, but the two had never related well to one another. As it turned out, Mr. Davies had died before father and son were able to reconcile their differences. The lack of resolution meant that Dick lived with gut-wrenching feelings of anger and frustration toward the memory of his father. Now here was this man, with whom he had

had such great conflict, imposing himself on the happy, independent life the young man had begun to create for himself.

Dick jumped up from his chair, shouting that he'd had enough. He grabbed the candle and blew at its flame to extinguish it. Much to the man's horror, his slight puff of breath not only did not extinguish the flame but rather provoked it to flare up angrily. As his wife and two friends watched in frightened amazement, he tried again. The flame enlarged to several centimetres in height and seemed to grow tentacles of fire. He set the apparently possessed candle back down on the table.

Janet, frightened and very much wanting to end this unnerving episode, then picked up the offending candle. As Dick had done only moments before, she blew at it to extinguish the flame. Oddly, the candlelight did not respond at all to the puff of air—a current of air that certainly should have been strong enough to put out such a candle. The flame simply burned, as though the air through it and around it was absolutely still. Thinking that she'd somehow misdirected her breath, Janice tried blowing on the candle a second and then a third time. Nothing happened. The flame burned on, completely undisturbed by her efforts to extinguish it.

Finally, in desperation, Al took the candle from Janet and blew the candle out, readily accomplishing what Dick and Janet had tried to do. Without a word, the two couples turned on the lights and retired to the Davies' living room. After a period of complete silence among the four, they began to piece together a possible scenario for the events that they'd just been involved in.

Clearly, Dick's father was an angry spirit. Whether his anger was over the many unresolved issues with his son or perhaps merely at having his peaceful afterlife disturbed, no one knew. The older man had died before Dick had met Janet, and so he had never known the woman who was now the mother of his grandchildren. If, in fact, it was his spirit controlling the candle's glow, then the difference between the firestorm kind of reaction to Dick's attempts to extinguish it as opposed to the complete calm for Janet, was interesting. As the angered entity had no emotional investment in Al, its spirit apparently didn't manifest itself in the candle and so the flame responded as it should have.

An hour later, the little group, Dick especially, remained uneasy. They wondered whether the spirit had left the apartment. It didn't feel as though it had, but perhaps it was only the memory of the spectre that lingered. Either way, the atmosphere was decidedly unpleasant. When Al and Barb invited their hosts to bring the children and spend the night downstairs in their apartment, Janet and Dick immediately accepted the invitation.

As Dick stood up to begin making the necessary preparations for the overnight stay away from home, Janet's teacup-turned-planchette suddenly began to move from where it had been resting at the centre of the dining-room table. With no one near it, but four pairs of eyes glued to its actions, the cup slid to the table's edge and inevitably crashed down on the hardwood floor, instantly breaking into almost exactly even quarters. Although no one said a word at the time, the incident certainly added to everyone's determination to take the children and leave the apartment.

Once in Al and Barb's apartment, the Davies and their children settled in as best as they were able to considering their makeshift accommodations. After a restless night they returned to their own apartment, where they found the atmosphere had, thankfully, returned to normal. They quickly swept the home-made Ouija board from the table into the garbage, and put the candle back on the sideboard where it had always sat.

The broken teacup, however, provided a bit more of a challenge. Even though it would never be functional again, the clean lines along which it broke meant that it could easily be glued back together if only for display. This possibility was a relief, because Janet could not bring herself to think of throwing the cup away. It had always been one of her favourites. Interestingly, it had been a gift from Dick's mother, the unwelcome spirit's widow.

The frightening seance was for a long time never mentioned among any of its unwilling witnesses. Years later, however, Barb and Al did have the opportunity to discuss it between themselves and with at least one other person. They concluded that they had, inadvertently, summoned the spirit of Dick's father; apparently against his will.

But what of the teacup? What unseen force had pushed it from the table? And why did it not shatter when it landed on the hardwood floor? Was there further significance in that it broke into four even pieces? It has since been suggested that the spirit and his namesake son who accidentally disturbed him both had first and last names beginning with the letter "D"—the fourth letter of the alphabet. That might be the explanation for that number of fragments, or it could have referred to there being four participants in the seance. As the pieces of the broken cup were almost exactly even, perhaps the spirit was implicating all four people in the disturbing incident.

Not surprisingly, none of the four ever attempted to partake in such a "game" again. In addition, the friendship that seemed to be forming before two couples entered into the impromptu seance never did develop. It was a decidedly strange experience for all who'd been a part of it. They were all as surprised that they were willing to indulge in such a dangerous pastime as they were by its results.

Some years later, in another part of Toronto, writer and freelance editor Dawn Hunter had a remarkably similar experience.

"When I was young, just after my grandfather died, my friends and I held a seance at Halloween. We sealed up the windows and put a towel under the door [to block any light that might have crept in]. We sat in a circle with a candle in the centre and held hands. I called for my grandfather, telling him that I had never had a chance to say goodbye. I felt very odd and asked for a sign. The candle flame shot up in the air! It scared us but I held the circle, said my goodbyes to him and we turned on the lights again. Everyone was pale and scared. We never did it again and we never talked about it again."

It is interesting that everyone involved in both the incidents immediately vowed never to do anything so potentially dangerous again.

Some Old-Fashioned Saskatchewan Stick Handling

Ottawa resident Don Wall's supernatural encounter was, without question, a life-saver. The incident occurred while he was staying by himself at his cottage on Rideau Lake for a few days in the fall of 1997.

"I had recently bought a 'float-boat,' which is much easier for an old guy like me to get on and off," he began. "I was heading into Portland, which is about two miles away, to a friend's to have some soup."

At this point in retelling the story, Don Wall paused for a moment and took a deep breath. "I ran out of gas about halfway there," he said simply.

"I had another tank of gas [in the boat] but both of my arms are rather crippled and I could not get the connection made [to refill the gas tank]. I had an anchor but no rope," Don chuckled.

Don realized that he was in a very serious situation. "I had nothing to do but drift. And drift I did. It was pitch dark and the wind was blowing. I had a bench at the back of the float-boat where I could lie down, but sleep was certainly out of the question. It was cold. All I had for a cover was two life-jackets. I draped one over my chest and one over my knees but they didn't help much. I started shivering very soon and drifted and drifted and drifted until, I guess, about 5 a.m. Then, *crunch*— I landed on a shoal."

Don continued, "I had a huge search light—a million candlepower—it's bright—[with] which I flashed around SOSs all over the place, but there wasn't a soul on the lake; not a boat, nothing. I was in a part of the lake [that] I guess is not very well populated anyway and surrounded by a sea of shoal markers."

The man knew his situation was becoming potentially lethal—not only was he stranded and in danger of developing hypothermia, but he was also weakened by his increasing hunger. All circumstances were conspiring against Don Wall coming through this misadventure alive.

"Then, God bless it, it started to snow," he recalled. "I ate the snow. It helped keep me alive but it didn't snow very long and so when it ran out I sort of staggered over to the edge and got some lake water and drank that. Well, I was shivering like crazy because I was freezing. It was at this point, I don't know whether I was hallucinating or not, but the devil appeared and said very firmly, 'I've got you now, you son of a bitch.'"

As emphatically and colourfully as he could, Don Wall told the devil to leave. "I was rather rude," he acknowledged.

"I want to talk to God," he informed the image, before imploring God's help directly. "I said, 'God, where are you when I need you?' And in a distant, almost female voice I heard quite clearly, 'Have faith and keep trying.'"

Even in these dire circumstances, Don showed his practical nature by replying, "Well, that's good advice, but who's going to fix these [crippled] arms of mine?' Besides, I was stuck on a shoal and even if the motor would run, I'd probably have crushed the propeller shaft so I just lay there till 4 p.m. thinking something's got to happen here."

Don called and called for help but there was no one to hear his pleas. He had no alternative but to accept the advice given by the mysterious, disembodied voice—he had to have faith that he would make it through this terrible ordeal alive and therefore he had to keep trying. He also brought to mind a philosophy that he'd learned years before while serving in the air force.

"I kept reminding myself, for God's sake, don't panic."

Once Don had calmed down sufficiently to think things through, he concluded, "This is going to require some old-fashioned Saskatchewan stick handling."

With that, he attempted what he had thought would be impossible considering his disabled arms. "I went back and leaned over the side and with all the pressure I could muster with both hands I finally got the connection [to the gas tank] but I thought, my battery's going to be dead by now anyway. I turned the key, left it in neutral and—it started!"

The boat's motor may have been running then, but the bottom of the craft was still grounded on the shoal.

"I tried—backward and forward, *crunch, crunch, bang, bang.*"

More determined than ever to heed the phantom voice's advice, he reasoned that there had to be some way to escape this apparent death-trap.

"I went back and leaned over the back [of the boat] at a precarious angle and looked to see just what rocks were holding me back. There was a huge one right beside the prop[eller] and I thought if I wheeled the motor around full to the right and backed it up I might just scrape by. I tried that and it went *crash, bang, crash, bang* and then suddenly it was quiet and I was moving. I got off the shoal but I wasn't quite sure where I was, where I'd drifted to. I headed in what I thought was a southeasterly direction. It was cold and threatening to snow again. I avoided a bunch of other shoals and finally spotted a familiar cottage, one that's only about three miles from home. I had been at least six-and-a-half miles from home—I'd drifted that far."

Don made it home safely that night, but to this day he credits the voice of the unseen presence with his rescue. Had he not heard those words of encouragement, he might not have persisted with the determination necessary to save himself. As it was, he barely made it into his boathouse. Fortunately, his motorized four-wheeler was there for him to drive up the hill to the life-giving warmth of his cottage. Once safely inside, the man made himself two strong drinks and a serving of warm soup and toast before crawling into bed and sleeping straight through for fourteen hours.

When he finally woke up, Don phoned his son, who immediately drove to the cottage to pick his father up and take him for a medical examination.

"I saw my doctor and she said, 'Well Don, you know I think you've come as close to hell as you're going to get without meeting it.'"

Little did the physician know how right she was.

Some days later, Don phoned his sister-in-law, Terry, in Australia. During the course of the conversation, he related the story of his terrible brush with death.

"I told her about the wispy female voice that said, 'Have faith and keep on trying.'"

Terry responded, 'Don, that wasn't God. That was [your] Mum.'

Don was intrigued by his sister-in-law's take on the identity of the disembodied voice. As he later explained to me, "She [Terry] was very close to my mother, as I was...."

After thinking about Terry's suggestion that the God-like voice he'd heard belonged to his deceased mother, he asked her, 'Terry, you're sure they're not one and the same?'

His sister-in-law conceded, 'I was never sure.'

The Team Reunited

Jim Lawrence sent me some wonderful ghost stories, but most of them took place in the province of Quebec and so could not be included in this book. The following one, however, took place in

Toronto and I'm so glad that it did, because just reading it gave me goose bumps!

"My grandfather [a man named George] died in Toronto in 1952. He was an iron-willed, dependable man who was the head of the family. Although strong, he was also a loving husband and father. My grandmother was a weak fiddle-faddler and they made a good team. [A long time a]fter my grandfather died, my grandmother was taken ill," Jim explained, and then added, as something of a foreshadow, "with some illness none of us could understand."

Jim continued, "She lay in a hospital bed in our dining room and was waited on hand and foot by my mother." This state of affairs continued for a year, and the older woman never did regain her health.

Jim's mother frequently sat with the ailing older woman as she lay sleeping. One night, around two in the morning, his mother heard the back gate slam closed. Although the sound startled her, she thought little of it and presumed that the wind had blown against it.

Immediately following the banging sound, however, she felt a distinct presence enter the room—the presence of Jim's long-deceased grandfather. The woman was comforted by the arrival of the man's presence, feeling that "all the responsibility for the night was off her shoulders and everything was all right."

The spirit's aura concentrated itself in an armchair in the corner of the room. Evidently, the seriously ill woman also felt the presence, for "she looked directly at the chair and said, 'George, George, it's been so long.'"

Both women's long vigils then ended as Jim's grandmother peacefully slipped from this life that very night.

A Fey Film Producer

Film producer Alice d'Anjou, who generously provided me with ghost stories that she'd collected over the years, has a special interest in paranormal phenomena. (See "Artifacts and Entities," p. 148; "Prime Minister Brought Spirit to Ottawa," p. 152; and "Mistress of the Mill," p. 225.) She explained, "I have always had a strong interest in ghosts, fairies, unexplained phenomena, etc. My Irish, very Catholic grandmother used to swear that I was 'fey' (possessing visionary power) and taught me at a very young age to trust my instincts no matter how silly it might feel at the time. She has proved to be right more times than I care to count. Whenever I do not listen to that little voice or that gut feeling, no matter how strange it may seem at the time, I usually regret it."

Alice continued, "Although I have never seen a ghost, I have developed a healthy respect for what I cannot see or understand. I have 'known' that my grandmother was looking out for me on several occasions when I needed a helping hand—just like she did all her life. I 'knew' to tell my best friend how much I loved her the last time I saw her before she died suddenly and unexpectedly. I have felt [my grandmother's] hand, her guidance, several times since then too. I 'knew' we would buy and love the house we live in now, days before I saw it. I 'knew' I should cleanse my new house with sweetgrass before moving anything into it, but that I would not need anything stronger. I found out later the previous owners had had a very bitter divorce but that the earlier history (it is eighty years old) was very good—only two previous families had grown up and flourished in it."

With these sorts of positive experiences listening to an unseen, unheard, but much-beloved presence, it's no wonder that one of Alice's recent film projects was about ghosts and haunted buildings.

The Seventh Child

There is nothing ordinary about Dawn Hunter, but then that probably could have been expected. She did not come from an ordinary family. Dawn explained to me that as children she, brother Scott and sister Karen spent their summers along with their mother, Mary Hunter, at the family cottage in the Haliburton area. One night her mother dreamt of a huge fire in the area—not long *before* it occurred. Another dream told Mary that her son Scott would happen upon a serious car accident. In her dream, she saw Scott staring into the twisted metal shell and being horrified by the sight of an apparently dead body inside the wreckage. Some time later, the accident occurred. Mary Hunter had, unconsciously, correctly predicted the terrible details—even that Scott, who arrived just after the accident had happened, was shocked and upset that the man inside the wreck was apparently dead. However, seconds later, the person inside the car spoke, which reassured Scott that the person wasn't dead after all and that his help would, fortunately, be necessary.

Dreams are not the only conduit through which Mary Hunter receives precognitive messages. The sensitive woman also reads tea leaves and tarot cards. One day she was giving a reading for a girl named Chris, her daughter Karen's friend. Poor Mary was shocked by what was at the bottom of the girl's cup. Dawn explained, "She saw demons, and 666, and flames and pain and the other symbols of evil."

Those dreadful visions might have ended the reading but they didn't end Mary's premonitions about Karen's friend.

Dawn continued, "Later that night she had a vision of my sister's friend being dragged away by a man, talked into something against her will."

These terrible visions were the first time that Mary had ever experienced this particular form of clairvoyance, and she was terrified by the negative scenes being played out in her mind. In a panic, Mary phoned Dawn and asked her to call Chris right away.

"Turns out that Chris had been getting interested in the occult and had been intrigued by a man she had met. He was in a coven. She was tempted to go to a meeting and was to meet him later that night. My mother begged her not to go, that he would force her into 'something,'" Dawn explained, before concluding the anecdote with the reassuring information, "Chris never went."

Mary was born and raised in Scotland. She was the seventh child of a seventh child—and credits that for her psychic abilities. But, as evidenced by the next chronicle, she has passed those abilities on to Dawn, who once accurately called the throw of two dice six times in a row.

On a more important level, Dawn once also psychically received a serious message from her sister.

"When [Karen] was living in Halifax and I was in Toronto, I had the strangest feeling that all was not well. I just knew something was wrong with Karen. I felt so sick and hot and just knew it was her. At that moment, we got a call from her fiancé telling us she was rushed to the hospital from work with toxic shock syndrome from, they [the doctors] believed, the solvents and glue where she was working."

Thankfully Karen recovered. Unfortunately, Mary's experience with *her* sibling did not end as positively.

Dawn recalled, "My mother was staying at my house for a few days. She was sleeping on the sofa bed. It was just after 2:30 a.m. and she was in quite a deep sleep. In the background she kept hearing a knocking sound...the kind that fits into your dream. It seemed like whoever was making the noise came and knocked directly on the open window by my mother's head." Apparently, Dawn's mother woke up, sat up and "as she pulled back the curtain she looked out. The porch seemed to be bright everywhere, lit up. She could see clearly."

What Mary Hunter saw next was even stranger than the knocking sounds she'd heard or the mysterious glowing light. There was a young man standing on the porch. His image was so solid and clear to her that she was later able to describe his clothing to Dawn and her husband. Oddly, though, the man's presence at the entrance to Dawn's house had not triggered the sensitive motion detectors that had been installed.

Afraid that the blonde, denim-clad man was an intruder, Mary called out for Dawn and her husband. The couple responded immediately and searched the entire house, but could not find any evidence that anyone had been there, although Mary continued to sense the young man's presence near her.

Dawn explained, "After we went back to bed she couldn't sleep. She looked out of the window and saw him on the porch again in that light. He waved to her and left."

Tragically the puzzle was solved the next day when Mary received a phone call from Scotland telling her that both her brother and his son, both named Andrew Thomson, had died the day before.

"Both men were tall and blonde. She suddenly realized that the figure on the porch looked like them [the two Andrews, whom she had not seen in many years]. Andrew Junior was in his forties and had died of a heart attack. He and my mother had been very close when he was a boy and he had visited us in Canada. When his father found him, he also died of a heart attack from the shock. We have often said that [appearing as the strange man on the porch] one or both of them were coming to say goodbye."

Mom Visits

Judy and her mother have always been close. So close that even the older woman's death only changed their relationship but could not destroy it. The first time that Judy became aware of the presence of her mother's spirit was not long after her mother died.

It was the late 1980s, an especially stressful period for both Judy and her husband, Ed.

"We moved up here, a little bit south of Timmins, from southern Ontario. The [paranormal] experiences began within a few months. It happened quite a bit the first couple of years I was here," Judy began.

She readily acknowledged that the transition from urban life to a rural setting was a difficult one for her.

"I think it was because of this extreme depression I was in. This was an adjustment period and I never really paid any attention to [the ghostly activity that she would regularly experience]. I often go to bed before my husband. [On one occasion] I was lying in bed and at first it felt like a cat jumping up on the bed. I wasn't asleep but I had my eyes closed and was very relaxed when I felt this. We didn't have a cat so I moved my legs. Between my knees and feet it just felt like something on the bed. I moved my legs because I really thought there was something on the bed or that Ed had sat down," Judy recalled.

The woman then sat up and quickly realized that she was completely alone in the room. This strange sensation of feeling a presence join her and yet not being able to see anyone, coupled with the depression that she had been suffering, initially made Judy keep her experiences a secret.

"I didn't say anything to anybody. I thought, oh, I'm losing my mind," she confided.

That first episode was only the beginning of Judy's encounters with the entity sitting on her bed.

At first the spirit came only at night. "Then it would happen at any time. For instance, sometimes if I would have a nap in the afternoon it would happen. I just sort of got used to it happening. Sometimes it would be on one side of the bed and sometimes it would be on the other. The first couple of years it was happening three or four times a week," Judy recalled.

As Judy adjusted to her new living conditions, the visits of the entity, whom Judy had come to recognize as her mother, to her bedside became less frequent, until they stopped altogether.

"Then, last April [1997] we renovated our house. We had seven bedrooms in our upstairs and we ripped it all out and made three bedrooms," Judy described.

Judy and Ed's master bedroom "moved from one side of the house to the other side. I had just lost a very very close friend to cancer. She had died virtually in my arms and then ten days after that I lost my uncle. So, I don't know, maybe someone was trying to comfort me because I was lying in bed and it happened again, not too long ago. I just thought, well, isn't that strange. I still keep on associating [the presence] with my mother.

Judy continued, "I think of [my mother] so often even though all these years have passed and especially when I'm going through some troubled times. I'll sit on the edge of my bed or I'll go up to my bedroom and I'll literally talk to her. You know like, 'Oh Mom, I'm having such a bad time.' I'll be crying and say, 'I wish you were here' and sometimes it happens," Judy explained, referring to the ghostly visits.

"I don't think I'm calling her to me but I don't know. It's very strange. It doesn't frighten me—not one bit," Judy asserted.

Finally, after years and years of experiencing visits from her long-deceased mother's spirit, Judy became comfortable enough with the encounters to share the news of their existence with her husband. She assured Ed, "It always happens when you're not here." Judy's mother has since also visited when Ed was also in the room, although he never became aware of the presence himself.

"It only ever happened once when he was in bed. He didn't feel it at all."

By now, Judy's not only comfortable with the visits from her mother, but she's actually comforted by them.

"At first it was a bit frightening because I didn't know what was happening but since then when it happens I feel like it's comforting. It's mother sending me a message."

And so, even though Judy's happily adjusted to her new life, she's still able to enjoy her deceased mother's companionship.

Chapter **4**

HISTORICALLY HAUNTED

Table Talk

Susanna Moodie was a pioneer settler in Ontario's mid-nineteenth-century wilderness. She, along with her sister, Catherine Parr Traill, and their brother, Samuel Strickland, immortalized themselves by their writings. Their books and essays left a dramatic picture of what life must have been like for immigrants from England. Susanna's writings also revealed her interest in what was then the current fad of spiritualism.

Initially a skeptic, Moodie, through her involvement in a number of seances, eventually became convinced that entities could manifest themselves to the living. During these seances, she heard phantom military music being played and witnessed both small and heavy objects being moved about a room by unseen forces.

These experiences bothered Susanna Moodie to the point that she began investigating them in the hope of finding matter-of-fact causes. As she contemplated what she'd been witness to, Moodie realized that she was beginning to accept the reality of paranormal experiences. This realization was so distressing to her that she spoke out loud and commanded the table she sat at to rise if it was, in fact, possible for the spirits of the dead to make contact with the living. The words were no sooner out of her mouth than an invisible force lifted the table and pushed it against her.

Moodie's husband, Dunbar, was so interested in the phenomenon that he constructed something he named a "Spiritoscope"—a device that could be considered to be a forerunner to the Ouija board. Encouraged by the table's responsiveness, Susanna immediately tried out the strange rudimentary communications device. Within moments, the spirit of a former colleague joined her in the room. The two communicated back and forth for some time, finally convincing Susanna Moodie that ghosts can, in fact, converse with the living.

The Donnellys Are Here

The story of Biddulph County's most infamous family is long, colourful, gruesome and extremely well documented. Songs, plays, articles and books have been written about the plight of the "Black Donnellys." Briefly, James and Johannah Donnelly, along with their one-year-old son, James Junior, arrived in what is now southwestern Ontario from their native Ireland in 1842. They had been poor in their homeland and were in even worse financial shape by the time they'd paid for and made their transatlantic voyage. The Donnellys made their way to a prime piece of unoccupied agricultural land near the town of Lucan and decided they'd found their new home.

No doubt delighted with their new surroundings, James and Johannah set about creating a life for themselves. They cleared the land, tilled the soil and constructed the necessary buildings. Unfortunately, they were so busy with the practical matters that they neglected to bother with the legal ones—they did not own the land on which they were now living and working.

Not long after the Donnellys began to reap the harvest of all their efforts, the acres they were squatting on were sold. The new owner wanted these interlopers off his land and was not willing to reimburse the Donnellys for the improvements they had made to it. Predictably, a lengthy, heated and tragic dispute broke out. A man named Pat Farrell was the first victim, killed by the elder James Donnelly during a drunken argument at a neighbour's barn-raising bee.

The elder Donnelly was tried, convicted of the murder and sentenced to death. The sentence was appealed and James eventually served a seven-year term in the Kingston Penitentiary. Those were tough years for all the Donnellys. Jail during the mid-1800s was not a place that would have improved anyone's outlook toward life, and at home Johannah and the eight Donnelly children, fending for themselves, were also becoming even more hardened than they had been. By 1865, James had paid his debt to society and the entire clan shared a decidedly bad attitude. They responded quickly and violently to every slight from the neighbours, whether it be real or imagined. Soon, nearly every family in the surrounding county had a bone to pick with the Donnellys. A feud of major proportions was brewing.

As with most feuds, proper judicial channels responded irritatingly slowly and, during the second month of 1880, a vigilante committee broke into the Donnelly home, murdered every family member at home at the time—James, Johannah, two sons and a niece—and then set fire to the place.

That mass murder marked the end of the Black Donnelly feud and the beginning of the Black Donnelly legend. As is fitting for folklore, the resulting stories are often considerably more colourful than reality. Perhaps that is why the myths continue to flourish. One of the most enduring of those stories is that all the

Jane Donnelly was always called Jennie. She's still a presence at the Donnelly place.

vigilantes who took part in the Donnellys' murders died violent deaths. Although somewhat vindicating, it is not true.

It is also said the Donnellys' apparitions have been seen floating above the fields they once farmed, and that it always rains in the cemetery where their remains lie. Other tales are equally imaginative and spooky. One legend indicates that horses refuse to go past the site of the massacre at midnight. On February 4 in particular, the anniversary of the murders, headless horses are seen galloping across the fields. And, on that same date, the phantom of a woman is seen on the road that runs past the old Donnelly place.

Although the chilling ghost stories surrounding the Donnellys may be fun, they are pale in comparison to the real ones.

In 1988 Rob and Linda Salts decided to make their dream of moving to the country a reality. In their search for a suitable rural property, they came across a real estate listing for a hobby farm near Lucan. The agent handling the property must have specialized in understatement, for he or she noted that the place had "an interesting history." That place was the former home of the infamous Black Donnellys.

The Salts moved in some months later and discovered, almost immediately, that in their newly purchased home the present could be every bit as "interesting" as the "history." Not surprisingly, the few acres of Donnelly land along the Roman Line and the buildings that remain there are well and truly haunted. They are so haunted, in fact, that when Rob Salts decided to write a book about his family's experiences living where the Donnellys once did, he called the book *You Are Never Alone*. Reading of his family's experiences and exchanging correspondence with the man certainly demonstrated to me that the title was well chosen.

Salts acknowledges that he is psychically sensitive and therefore became aware of the spirits around the old place almost as soon as the family began to move their possessions onto the property. He explained, "While unloading and carrying items into the barn I had the eerie sensation of being watched. With each trip up to the homestead, I felt that eeriness build. It was as if I were surrounded by unseen residents in the barn."

Given that the barn predates the terrible massacre, his experience really wasn't too surprising. In order to understand what he was feeling, Rob relaxed enough to receive the psychic messages more clearly. As shapes began to form in his mind, Rob explained that he felt crowded to the point that he wanted to bolt from the barn.

Since then, visitors to the place have reported similar feelings. Two students confided that while enjoying Rob's tour of the property they both felt pressure on their chests specifically while they were in the barn, and one added that she'd experienced clairaudient (intuitively heard) screams from the barn. Other tourists have reported similar feelings.

Rob's wife, Linda, was the next to detect feelings that she wasn't entirely comfortable with. Rather than in the barn, Linda's unpleasant experiences occurred in the kitchen. The middle section of their house dates back to 1881, just after the massacre, and was actually built by James and Johannah's son William, who had survived the lethal raid because he'd been living away from home at the time. By coincidence, when rebuilding, William had chosen the site where his father had built the original shanty in 1845. In honour of the five murdered members of his family, William planted five horse chestnut seedlings. Today, two of those seedlings, now strong, healthy trees, remain as valued enhancements to the Salt family's property.

Linda Salts reacted to the atmosphere inside the home with vague, unspecified feelings of depression. The couple discussed the situation and decided to call in a Catholic priest. Although the Salts are not of that faith, they knew that the Donnellys had been. Stopping short of offering an actual exorcism, a priest did come and bless the house and offered last rites to whatever spirit remained in the kitchen. This last ceremony was profoundly moving for everyone involved and, over the course of the weeks that followed, the feelings of heaviness that had made Linda so uncomfortable began to lessen until they were, according to Rob, "conspicuous by their absence."

The Salts' son, Charles, was five years of age when the family moved to their "new" home. In common with many children, Charles was able to see manifestations that the adults did not.

One morning, while playing in his bedroom, he observed a man and a woman dressed in plain black clothes and accompanied by two children wearing lacy white outfits standing in his room. He immediately ran to report the sighting to his parents. Rob recalled that, although the child was clearly excited by what he'd seen, he was not seriously distressed.

Rob has also seen apparitions, although not as clearly as those seen by young Charles. On one occasion, he was taking a shower when the shadow of a human shape fell across the shower curtain. Instantly he pulled the curtain back—only to find that he was as alone in the room, as he'd originally thought.

Even visitors to the place, people merely waiting for Rob to take them on his popular historical tour, have reported seeing what they take to be living people darting about the property. Rob patiently informs the visitors that they have just seen a ghost.

While those experiences have all been fleeting, some of the spirit presences in the former Donnelly home are constant. For instance, one smoke detector, which has purposely been left without a battery, will beep intermittently, most frequently between the hours of one and six in the morning.

Phantom noises also occur, including the sounds of footsteps on the stairs heard after everyone in the household has gone to bed for the night. A voice will sometimes call out the name of a member of the Salt family so clearly that that person will check to see which of the others has called out, only to be informed that no one was calling him or her.

Once, when passing an empty outbuilding on the property, Linda heard the sound of someone inside sawing. She was the only one home at the time and the outbuilding was locked— from the outside.

For sheer intensity, the apparently sourceless crashing sound they hear is difficult to beat. Rob Salts described the sound as similar to that which a car hitting a house might make. Because the Salts first heard the awful noise in the winter, they surmised that it might have been caused by ice sliding off one section of the roof onto the part directly above their bedroom. Any comfort the pair got from accepting that theory disappeared the first time they heard the noise during the summer. The experience was even more distressing when they realized that the tremendous noise defied a law of physics by being vibration-free.

At least one of the manifestations on the property seems to be continuing, over one hundred years later, to be carrying out his or her routine from life: an entity is heard coming up to and then opening the door of the house. As well, in typical ghost style, the presences around the Salts' historical home like to play with light switches and torment the Salts' dog, who absolutely refuses to use either staircase in the house. The spirits are also implicated in tools or other supplies temporarily going missing.

When a psychic contracted by the Arts & Entertainment television network went through the house, she detected a female entity whom she felt was Jennie, the Donnellys' only daughter. Other psychics visiting the property with film crews have described two other "stern-looking" spectres—one a tall man with a beard and homespun clothing, the other a woman with her hair worn in a bun. She is wearing a plain dress and high button shoes. These are likely the spirits of Johannah and James Donnelly, who apparently have been unable to completely leave the property they gave their lives for.

The Donnellys need not worry though, for their land and the legend that their lives became are being carefully attended to by the Salts family. The Salts thoroughly enjoy not only living on the unique property but sharing their knowledge and enjoyment with interested visitors from all over the world.

"A Ghastly Apparition"

The Niagara Falls area may be Ontario's most haunted area. The following account dates back to November 22, 1880, demonstrating that Niagara's haunted heritage is long and colourful:

The town of Niagara is in a state of excitement over a ghastly apparition [that] has haunted the place of late. The experiences are growing more numerous and even men are chary of going abroad after dark. A farmer leaving town the other night about eleven o'clock, the moon being bright, avers that he saw the thing rise from among the tombs in the churchyard and trail toward him. It had the semblance of a woman with long white garments and fair hair, apparently floating or else with far more than the average length of limb. The farmer closed his eyes and, turning his horse, drove back into town at a furious gallop, his animal seeming to share the fright. He never looked round until safely in the heart of the town. Another account states that at one of the lonely crossings in the outskirts of the place the woman was seen crouching beside a low fence. The spectators, two in number this time, did not at first recall the stories of the apparition and went toward the thing under the impression that some vagrant was crouching there for shelter. As they near a peculiar sensation affected them both and without speaking to each other or exactly knowing why they stopped involuntarily and turned away. As they did so a shuddering thrill went through them, as they say, and they broke into a wild run for the nearest lights.

Other tales have contradictory points but all agree that the apparition has the form of a woman and possesses a strange floating motion. There is much speculation in the place over the matter.

Five successful burglaries have been accomplished and three unsuccessful ones attempted and the evil deeds are still going on. It is possible that the burglaries have been committed by the ghost although there is nothing to show this positively.

All in the Family

In 1853, after a five-year courtship, Chief George Johnson and Emily Howells married. Johnson was an important and influential member of the Six Nations Iroquois Confederacy and, like his father, he had chosen to marry a woman of British descent. Determined that his beloved Emily would never want for anything, Johnson immediately began drawing up plans for "Chiefswood," the majestic family home situated on 81 hectares of land along the Grand River. This mansion of Johnson's design, at 195 square metres, quickly became a proud focal point of the reserve. The house also became the birthplace of one of Canada's greatest and most prolific poets—E. Pauline Johnson. Her signature work, *The Song My Paddle Sings*, remains a

Canadian classic even today. The palatial home in which Pauline Johnson was raised still stands, now as a museum on only 1.6 hectares of land. And it is occasionally haunted.

Sheila Johnston, Pauline's most recent biographer, is the educational coordinator of the very haunted Grand Theatre in London, Ontario. While one of her colleagues at the theatre advised me of Sheila's book about the poet, another indicated that, as I was collecting ghost stories, I should ask Sheila about an experience she'd had at Chiefswood. Some weeks later I enjoyed a long conversation with the author of *Buckskin and Broadcloth*.

"In September 1995, CBC reached me after reading an article in the *Globe and Mail*. I [took] the CBC crews to Chiefswood because they wanted some on-site interviewing done," Sheila Johnston began.

"[Veteran CBC journalist] Dan Byarnesson and I were getting ready for the interview. We were in Chiefswood. I was wearing a body mike [a small and unobtrusive microphone pinned to a person's clothing] and Dan was [also] wearing a body mike. Apparently the sound technicians thought [that these microphones] would be fine and so we started the interview. We didn't get very far when the sound man said, 'I'm not picking up Dan Byarnesson.' He checked Dan's microphone and, according to the sound man, it was a fine working microphone. He said to try it again, so we started the interview a second time," Sheila Johnston recalled.

The second attempt was cut short almost immediately with a loud and emphatic "no" from the frustrated audio technician. He announced that Dan's mike wasn't working and that he'd go out to the truck, where he had a second body mike to replace the "faulty" one.

Sheila explained that once the man had swapped the microphones, the aborted interview began again.

Chiefswood Museum is occasionally visited by Eva Johnson, sister of legendary poet E. Pauline Johnson.

"Nope!" cried the sound technician, cutting off this third attempt to record the interview. "I can't hear Dan," he said.

"By now everybody was starting to get perturbed," biographer Johnston explained. Everyone, that is, except Sheila herself.

Over the course of the years that she'd been researching and writing her book about Pauline Johnson, Sheila had become very aware that not all the personalities that once formed the nucleus of the poet's family had left this world. And, on the day of the interview, she was convinced that the spirit of Eva, Pauline's sister, was interfering with the production.

"I thought, this is typical, so typical, because there are forces afoot that, in the past, made sure that my interviews had not gone smoothly," Sheila reflected.

"Finally the sound man, completely exasperated by this time, said, 'Fine. If body mikes aren't going to work we'll have to go back to the old-fashioned boom [mike].' He sort of stomped out to the sound van and brought back this boom and he held it over Dan's head. Finally he said, 'now I think we'll get our sound.'"

The connection between ghosts and things electrical and electronic is well documented, but if so, why would the ghost of Eva Johnson just prevent the reporter's mike from functioning and not Sheila Johnston's as well?

"I believe a spirit at Chiefswood was saying, 'We don't mind Sheila being here but, darn it, who are all these CBC people? They're very intrusive and this is not pleasant at all,'" Sheila said.

It was interesting that Sheila Johnston had never considered the possibility that the presence was that of Pauline herself.

"I think Pauline's spirit is at rest," Sheila attested. "Eva is quite active. I had foreknowledge [of Eva's presence]... my partner Raymond and I were at CBC radio in Vancouver in the fall of 1994. We went on the Vicky Gabereau Show [and] the producer took us to the studio. We conducted what we thought then was an uninterrupted interview. Only after we got back to Ontario did the producer phone and say, 'I have to phone you because something's happened that's never happened before. We were taping you, it was reel-to-reel [tape] and it was working perfectly, but you came to a part in the interview where you said that you were going to recite a lost poem by Pauline Johnson you felt was a poem written by Pauline that reflected herself and her sister,'" Sheila related, recalling the reading. The producer then informed her that "halfway through the poem, the reel-to-reel [tape recorder] slowed down to a halt. The sound man went nuts because at no time during his whole CBC career had such an event occurred."

Sheila explained, "I'm sure that Evelyn [Eva] Johnson was the one who was not happy that day that I introduced the poem and that I used her name."

But Pauline Johnson's sister is not the only spirit that Sheila thinks visits Chiefswood every now and again.

"George [Pauline's father] had died in that home. As the family patriarch he may have been very exasperated with the CBC crew."

The ghost's identity may be open to some speculation, but its attitude toward intruders with recording devices in the proud and grand old family home was clear.

Fort George Has Ghosts Aplenty

The "ghost tours" at Fort George in Niagara-on-the-Lake were created several years ago by historic interpreter Kyle Upton. Like everyone associated with the fort, Kyle had heard lots of old stories about it being haunted. His background is science, so he had always tended to be a disbeliever. Skepticism aside, the special tours seemed like a unique way in which he could share his love of the old fort with the thousands who came to visit the historic site each year. From today's perspective, it's clear that the personable young man's hunch was a good one. The tours have proven to be very popular—both with the living and with the long-deceased.

"Over the years of ghost tours, the spirits have provided us with a variety of new stories. Of the fifteen stories on this year's tour, only two are more than five years old," Kyle began. The other thirteen stories are about ghosts who have manifested themselves since he began drawing visitors' attention to the other-worldly residents at Fort George.

The place, Kyle explains, is now a National Historic Site. "[It was] built on the ruins of a British fortification that saw service as a military headquarters and supply base during the War of 1812. During the war the fort and nearby town [Niagara-on-the-Lake] were shelled fairly regularly from the American side. If you need suffering, pain, hatred and death for there to be ghosts, then history makes it clear why Niagara claims the title of being the most haunted town in Canada."

One of the most dramatic additions to the tour is associated with Blockhouse 1.

"When I started doing the tours in 1994, I had nothing spooky to say about Blockhouse 1. Throughout the first year of ghost tours, however, I would regularly have visitors comment about a shadowy figure seen standing in a ground-floor window, staring at the tour as it went in. I also would hear tales about a figure that was seen to pace back and forth behind that same window. I had one entire group of eighteen- to twenty-four-year-old couples refuse to leave the fort for a considerable time as more than half the group had seen this figure," Kyle explained. "There is nothing more disturbing than having a half dozen twenty-year-old guys who, up until this point had been playing the macho 'don't worry honey, I'll save you from the spooky ghosts' game with their girlfriends, suddenly freaking out, jumping straight past macho and into fight-or-flight mode!"

Despite such occasional dramatic audience reactions, Kyle still wasn't convinced that whatever people were reacting to couldn't be explained.

"The light in the fort at night can play tricks with your eyes and the power of suggestion is a wonderful thing," he reasoned initially. His confidence, born of disbelief, didn't last. "Two years later, I changed my story. Now, the fort at night can be an intimidating place, even for those familiar with it. There are some nights when it even gets to me. It doesn't bother me when I'm leading the tours—usually—as I have the safety of the lantern and thirty or so rapt ghost 'tourites' between me and the darkness, but once the paying customers escape to the safety of their cars, I have to slink back into the fort to close up for the evening. It is then, with the hour of midnight fast approaching and the depths of darkness settled about the ramparts, that the atmosphere of the fort changes from that of a tourist attraction to that of a churchyard. The air thickens to the point of oppressiveness and a haze settles into the corners of your vision, only to vanish as you turn to confront it. [One night] as I sped to escape from what had become a less-than-comfortable Fort George, I looked up into the lit window of Blockhouse 1 only to find its light occluded by the shadowy form that filled the aperture."

Kyle continued, "Now, I'd seen ghosts before and I'm not spooked easily, but while other ghostly experiences had been curious sensory phenomena, this one hit me at a purely emotional level. I was filled with such a gut-level feeling of terror that I contemplated climbing over the ten-foot-high palisades to escape from the fort rather than risk walking past that building to the front gate. Thankfully, when I'd recovered my nerve, after cowering in the brightly lit staff building, and ventured once more into the darkness, the apparition was gone," Kyle explained. "He [it?] hasn't bothered me since. I do not know whether this is because I now tell his story with respect and perhaps a certain amount of fear or because I now take pains not to look into that window when I walk through Fort George after the sun has set."

Kyle's close friend and co-worker, William Foster, has not been so fortunate, however.

"[It was] August 19, 1997...William Foster's last day in Ontario before he headed back to Montreal. He's had a whole year [now] to think about what happened. At the time he was in no proper state to tell us what happened. He had enjoyed a fabulous summer working at Fort George, and he was sad that he had to leave so early in August. When he had first heard that there were ghost tours at Fort George he had assumed that [they] involved actors who dressed up in old clothing and scared the tourists. He was amazed to find that some of the staff members he had come to know and respect over the summer were actually naive enough to believe that ghosts actually exist," Kyle recalled. "With William's background in science and particularly physics, he knew that ghosts were simply childish fantasies, the result of over-active imaginations. He had gone on the staff ghost tour earlier in the season and he simply hadn't computed what kind of atmospheric phenomena could have caused [the assortment of reported mysterious events] but it certainly couldn't have been a ghost—there was definitely some normal explanation."

Kyle continued, "So, after bidding farewell to the [other] staff, William returned to Fort George in the darkness, for a final ghost tour. As the tour headed out of the fort, William turned to bid a final farewell to the fort he'd come to love. With perhaps a tear in his eye he turned to go but stopped when he heard a footstep on the gravel off to his right. Peering into the darkness he called out, 'who's there?' as another footstep crunched on the gravel from the direction of the lit ground-floor window of Blockhouse 1. William called out to the tour leader that there was something weird going on but the tour was too far away to hear [him] as another footstep scratched the earth, coming closer. As the footsteps came closer they got faster. A quick walk, closer, trot, closer still, run, sprint, closer still and then he described this thing [that] just suddenly sped up. It was like something came steam-rolling or leaping toward him. Paralysed by a mixture of fear and curiosity, it was too late for him. He threw his arms up in front of his face, tumbling backward onto the ground, crying out in startled terror. As members of the tour returned to see if he was all right, William sensed, through some combination of hearing and feeling, this thing retreating from his approaching rescuers, not back to the building from whence it came but off into the darkness between the buildings. Free to lurk, beyond the candlelight, in the shadows of the fort."

Kyle acknowledged, "I've never seen anyone so freaked out. We had a hard time because then we had to come back in to lock up the fort. We told him 'you can either wait outside the fort by yourself in the dark or you can come back in.' He decided to come back in just to be with the group but...he had the Maglite [flashlight] in his hand and he swears the whole time that we walked about the fort that there was a figure in the building sort of jokingly waving at him. He'd say, 'Look, can't you see it? Can't you see it?' And we'd look over at the window and of course we couldn't see anything but he swears that this thing was mocking him."

Thankfully, Kyle added, "William recovered from his experience, and he still considers Fort George [to be] one of his favourite places but the last thing he said to me as I saw him to the bus the next morning was, 'Kyle, I went on two of your ghost tours. I went in as a complete skeptic and, well, I'm not [a] skeptic now. And you know, I think the tours are great but you have to promise me that you will never take a group into that building because there are some things in Fort George that don't like us in their fort.'"

Kyle has heeded his friend's admonition.

And so, while "suffering, pain, hatred and death" might not always be necessary ingredients in a haunted place, at Fort

George they have clearly combined to result in at least one spirit who is not receptive to visits from the living.

Not all the ghost stories from Fort George are quite that frightening, however. Irving, for instance, is a most benign presence.

"Irving's a gentleman who's been seen in the upper floor of the soldiers' barracks building, so presumably he was a soldier. He makes sort of a nuisance of himself sometimes, with odd noises and moving things about, but mostly I guess he's just seen."

Oddly, Kyle himself has never seen this particular apparition, but neither he nor William doubt the manifestation's existence in Fort George at Niagara-on-the-Lake.

Enduring Screams

Burlington may hold bragging rights to the most enduring Ontario haunting. Given the circumstances under which Jem Horner died, it's not surprising that his spirit continues to scream out, frightening those passing by.

The year was 1830. Horner and many like him managed to eke out a meagre living in the shipping trade that flourished on the Great Lakes. The work was dangerous and only the strongest scowmen survived. Personal toughness was considered a valuable asset, a pleasing personality was not. Although Jem Horner was remembered as being a cruel and hateful person, it was not these characteristics but the shipping life that led Horner to his demise.

While helping to unload a barge, Horner slipped between the vessel and the dock. He pulled himself up as quickly as he could. Seconds later, when the next wave jostled the heavily laden boat against the dock, one of Jem Horner's legs remained in harm's way. The man shrieked in agony—his limb pulverized by the force.

Jem's co-workers were not without compassion. They carried him to an abandoned house nearby but, as he was anything but popular with his colleagues and there was still a substantial amount of profitable cargo to be off-loaded, that was all that the other men did for the injured man. They left him there alone, moaning and crying out in pain.

That evening a passer-by, whose name has, by now, been lost, heard the man's cries for help and investigated. Seeing the dreadful condition of the man, this good Samaritan ran all the way to Hamilton and begged a doctor, now known only as "Dr. Case," to come and see the suffering Jem Horner.

By the time the rescuer and the doctor arrived back, Horner was maddened by pain and the crushed leg was well beyond saving. Amputation in that era, especially under such circumstances, offered little hope, but Case apparently determined that the patient was sure to die if the damaged limb was left attached. He began the procedure. Despite the life-saving attempts, Horner, still in agony, died later that night.

It is said that the one-legged spirit of Jem Horner still wanders the area around the Burlington Canal. For years afterward, the ghostly cries from that tortured soul could be heard coming from the abandoned house in which he died. In an attempt to rid the area of the terrifying sounds that the presence created, the long-deserted building was eventually torn down.

As recently as 1978, however, when the location of the terribly haunted house was still remembered by old-timers in the area, some swore that when they passed by they could still hear "blood-curdling screams" echoing through the night air.

The Witch of Plum Hollow

The "Witch of Plum Hollow" is one of the most colourful pieces of southeastern Ontario folklore. The person around whom the legend revolves, also known as "Mother Barnes," lived roughly twenty kilometres south of Smiths Falls and was apparently internationally recognized as having psychic powers. She was the seventh daughter of a seventh daughter and, for a small fee, the Irish immigrant of Spanish descent would read fortunes. On a more practical note, she would advise farmers as to where they could find cattle that had wandered off their property.

However, it was a murder that caused Elizabeth Barnes' reputation to become firmly ensconced in the esteem of her community. In 1860, men seeking the answer to a colleague's disappearance consulted the sixty-year-old woman in her log house. The details of the murder case have become confused with the passing of years, but it seems that a pair of cousins from England, Morgan Doxtater and Edgar Harter, had settled in the area. In the fall of 1860, one of them disappeared and the other reported that his cousin had accidentally drowned. Some of the missing man's friends were suspicious of the survivor's story. They took their concerns to the one person they knew could see through the "veil of the past" and let them know the truth.

As the men walked toward her house, the psychic greeted them by saying, "You have come here regarding the death of a man." Immediately after that, the deceased's spirit came to the "witch" and told her where his body was hidden and how he had died. She related the information to the men, and they took the news to the local authorities. The surviving cousin was tried and convicted of murder based on a communication from beyond the grave.

A Government Ghost

We don't usually associate government offices with ghosts, but occasionally our country's bureaucrats have been known to share their offices with those from the spirit world. A two-hundred-year-old former home in Windsor now houses offices—and ghosts.

"This area is one of the oldest English-speaking settlements west of Montreal," explains communications spokesperson Sandra Bradt, assistant general manager and director of group tour marketing for the City of Windsor.

The haunted building in this story is one of the oldest buildings in this already historically significant setting.

After I agreed to protect his identity, an employee in the haunted office spoke freely with me about his ghostly experiences at work. By now "Ken" (a pseudonym) is quite used to working in a haunted building. He and other employees are accustomed to the ghosts occasionally playing practical jokes—such as when the staff arrive in the morning and unlock the well-secured building to find the books on their office shelves turned upside down.

And Ken is certainly not the only one working there who is aware of the supernatural forces in the place. One morning "Tom" (another pseudonym) arrived at work and heard water gushing in the basement. He didn't immediately relate the noise to the ghost, but presumed instead that the sump pump had broken.

"We have had trouble with the basement flooding," said Ken, explaining that this interpretation of the sounds was Tom's first thought. There had been a lot of rain in the area recently and so the man made his way to the basement, expecting to find it flooded. Much to his surprise, there was not a drop of water anywhere, the sump pump was working well and the sounds of water running had stopped. Assured that there was no problem, Tom went back up to his office.

He had no sooner sat down at his desk when the sounds of water running started again. Not content this time to check just the basement, the concerned worker made a thorough search of the entire building, but he didn't discover the source of the phantom sounds.

One of the administrative assistants, a woman whose office is adjacent to Ken's, has something of a "trick" door to her office. Periodically, when no one's near it, the door to this woman's office will simply slam closed.

"While she is working her door will slam shut. It's happened when she's been by herself, it's happened when she's had clients in her office, and it's happened when one of the other consultants that works in the building has been there. And it slams, it doesn't close. It slams when there's no wind, none," Ken noted.

It would be interesting to know whether the spirit is shutting something in or out of the small room.

Ken went on to explain that there is no question as to whether these office ghosts might possibly be associated with one or more of the workers and not the facility itself.

"During the restoration [of the building, some]one was giving tours of [the house]. She'd finished the main floor tour and they were on their way up [to the second floor]. The staircase goes up and sort of does a landing and then you go to the right. [The tour guide] got up to the landing and was turning the corner and she said there was something stopping her. She said she had a strong sense that somebody was [there who] wouldn't let her go any further. She said that the hair [on her neck] stood up on end and she felt cold and clammy and she turned and said 'I don't think it's safe that we go any further on the tour' and turned around and went back."

It seems that the ghost was dictating the itinerary of the tour—for that day, at least.

Another incident that occurred before a group of people happened at an evening meeting in which Ken was involved.

"One night I had a meeting in the boardroom and there were about six gentlemen with me. The house is alarmed so if you were to come in the door it would go *beep-beep*. There were only probably eight of us in the meeting and we were all on the main floor. During the meeting somebody [else] walked across the second floor," he stated simply. "Now I heard it as clear as you and I are talking. Other people heard because you could tell that they heard it. The meeting went on; then there was a pause and one of the guys said, 'I thought we were the only ones in the house' and I said, 'yes, we are.' About three of them immediately turned on me and said, 'Who are you trying to fool? We heard somebody walk across the floor upstairs.' I said, 'Well, there is nobody else in this building,' and they said, 'We heard it.' I said, 'Well, one go up the back stairs and one go up the front stairs and go and check it out if you don't believe me.' So off they went and of course they couldn't find anything. They came back down and then we heard a door close and more footsteps—[the ghost had] left."

At least for that phantom visit, Ken had company, unlike the time he was alone in the building, trying to finish up some work.

"I was on the main floor doing some photocopying, facing the photocopier. Behind me is the entry way to the basement as well as one of the main doors to the facility. The hair on the back of my neck stood up—that feeling that someone's standing behind you and you haven't heard them; they're just standing there. It was very very very strong and I turned around and, of course, there's nothing there. As crazy as this sounds, I said, 'I've got about five more minutes of photocopying and then I'm going to be leaving and the house will be yours.' I turned back [to face the copier] and I did [the rest of my work] and I didn't have the feeling any longer. I've had many of those experiences—in the daytime as well as in the evening."

When Ken had to work in the evenings, he often took his dog, a ten-year-old golden Labrador named Buddy, to the office with him for company. Like most animals, Buddy was much more able to sense spirits than are humans.

"I'd bring him in the evenings and he would always start to pant when we got to the door. When we came into the house he definitely wanted to leave. There were very clear indications that Buddy wanted out of the house. There was one time I was on the main floor in what we call our kitchen and Buddy was panting. He would look at me and then he would look out the window— the window's venetian blind was closed. Then he'd look back at me and sort of whine and look back at the window and I knew him well enough that he was trying to tell me something. He did that several times and although I knew that there was nothing behind the window, that I could see, he certainly was telling me there was something. So I quickly opened up the venetian blind to [try to] catch someone looking in [through] the window and of course there was no one there."

Ken went on to describe what would often happen on those evenings when he worked late. "My office is up on the second floor. [Buddy] would come in and he would lie at the side of the desk so I could see him. I'd be working at the computer and he would start to pant again. He would look at me and look over at the doorway and I could tell again that he was sensing something. Of course, I would look at the doorway and there wouldn't be anything there but I would equally have a very very strong sense that somebody was standing in the doorway looking at me."

Given the building's lengthy history, it's difficult to even guess who the ghost or ghosts might be. "I do get the sense that it is a small person—a hunched-over man. That's my sense. I sense there's two, both male and female. The woman I see in pilgrim clothes. I've never seen her but that's the sense I get," concluded Ken.

And so, in the oldest section of Windsor, Ontario, the deceased and the living work together with minimal disturbances between the two realms.

Bewitched, Cursed or Haunted?

The following story is widely known as the "Baldoon Mystery" and is probably the most enduring ghost story from Ontario's history. The intensity of the paranormal activity in the tiny settlement of Baldoon must have been terrifying, not only for the family involved but for all the settlers there. The manifestations they witnessed and experienced were classically poltergeist-like in nature; they were often violent and occasionally life-threatening. Yet there is some question as to whether the events were perpetrated by a ghost or by some other supernatural means. Unfortunately, we will probably never know. We can only be sure that the fear provoked by the ghostly activity was certainly sufficient to warrant finding a scapegoat—and that is just exactly what might have happened in this chronicle of a haunting. In 1829, when the frightening activity began at the home of John and Nancy MacDonald, the hamlet of Baldoon, near Lake St. Clair (not far from present-day Wallaceburg), had been established for only twenty-five years. The residents of Baldoon were Selkirk settlers—Scots who, in the early 1800s, ventured out into the New World under the auspices of the Earl of Selkirk. Most villages of Selkirk settlers flourished. For reasons probably unconnected with the ghost story, this particular one did not, and all that now remains of the community of Baldoon is a roadside plaque.

At the time of the haunting, however, Baldoon was a village of hard-working Scottish immigrants who devoted their lives to farming the land that they'd been assigned. Although they undoubtedly missed Scotland, few who came could ever have hoped to own property if they'd stayed behind. The adults in the group must have known when they made the decision to emigrate that there would be difficult times ahead, but likely none of them anticipated the terror that they were about to face as forces that they could not understand invaded their serenity.

It began one fall night in 1829 when Mr. and Mrs. MacDonald were sleeping peacefully. Mrs. MacDonald was the first to hear the noises. It sounded as though an intruder had broken into their home. She awakened her husband and together they listened as the sound of footsteps roamed through their home. They kept still and quiet, praying that the burglar would take what he wanted and leave without hurting any of them, for the MacDonalds' two young sons, a baby daughter and a teenage foster daughter slept in rooms nearby. After only a few moments, however, one of the children called out and the MacDonalds bolted from their bed, knowing that they would have to risk encountering the robber.

Mrs. MacDonald went directly to the crying child's room while Mr. MacDonald searched the house for the noisy intruder. He must have been as confused as he was relieved when he found that there was no one in the house who shouldn't have been there. Little did the family know at the time that this night was only the beginning of what was to be three terror-filled years.

The sounds of phantom footsteps throughout their home soon became frighteningly routine for the MacDonalds. They agreed not to discuss the unexplained noises with anyone in the community. After all, if they couldn't understand the phenomenon themselves, they would certainly have difficulty explaining it to others, especially if they wanted to avoid being ridiculed by their neighbours.

Soon the apparently sourceless footsteps began to be heard during the day as well. It was only a matter of time, the MacDonalds knew, before neighbours would be visiting when the invisible presence walked about. They were right. They had also been correct in assuming that it wouldn't take long for word of the extraordinary sounds to spread throughout the closely knit community.

While the footsteps continued, the intensity of the haunting increased. The next display of poltergeist-like tricks took place in the family's barn. Some of the girls from the neighbouring farms had gathered there to attend to chores that would have to be done before the winter set in. The MacDonalds' foster daughter, Jane, was one of those girls. The girls chatted and giggled as they worked, making a social occasion out of the mundane tasks. Without warning, a beam from the barn's roof fell into their midst. Amazingly, no one was hurt.

Not knowing what else to do, the young women continued on with what they had been doing. No sooner had they restarted their work when a second beam fell. At this, the young women began to investigate. They checked all around the barn and determined that there was no one other than themselves in there. They also climbed up to examine the remaining beams. All seemed to be sturdy and secure. Assured by the results of their investigation, the girls once again resumed their chores. Seconds later a third beam fell from the roof. Terrified, they fled to the nearby farmhouse.

There, in the MacDonalds' kitchen, the youngsters composed themselves before relating the strange and frightening events that had just occurred to them in the barn. The concerned adults had little time to assess what they were hearing. Suddenly, a lead bullet pierced a nearby window, and then another and another, until three windows had been punctured by bullets.

Photos of the house and the barn where the "Baldoon Mystery" took place.

The group rushed outside to see if they could spot the careless hunter who had fired the rounds, but there was no one about— no one visible anyway. The terrifying haunting had now begun in earnest. Bullets continued to drill neat holes through the glass windows in the house—the glass never shattered as it should have. Each spent bullet landed harmlessly on the floor without doing any additional damage.

John MacDonald eventually became fed up with the expense of replacing the panes and resorted to boarding up the windows in his house. That strategy did save him having to replace the glass, but it did nothing to stop the hail of bullets. They continued to whiz dangerously into the house but most, oddly, never made a hole in the wooden planks that he had nailed in place over the windows.

The entire community was puzzled and frightened. No one had any idea what strange forces they were dealing with. Everyone was on the lookout for the perpetrator of these bizarre and dangerous stunts. Spotting the culprit, if there had been a visible one, shouldn't have been difficult, for the MacDonald property lay in a clearing with no place for a person to hide. The missiles, now in the form of stones as well as bullets, continued to invade the house and the ghostly footsteps continued to sound, both seemingly by some kind of evil magic.

Neighbours gathered to offer suggestions to the beleaguered family in the haunted house. One man present that day, a skeptic, was hit by a projectile while he was visiting. Angered, he ordered whatever force was in control to throw another stone his way. This one he said he would catch. As though whatever was to blame for the disturbances not only heard but understood the man's exhortation, a second, larger stone shot toward the man. Now frustrated and frightened as well as angry, the man took the second piece of rock and threw it into the nearby river.

Moments later the same stone, now wet and muddy, reappeared in the house. It seemed that the malevolent supernatural power was possessed of intelligence.

The invisible and evil energy was increasing in strength. As a crowd that had gathered at the home watched in horrified silence, a tiny cradle where the MacDonalds' baby lay sleeping began to rock. The motion became so violent that Mrs. MacDonald snatched the child from the bed just before she would have been thrown to the floor. No one could see any source for the sudden movement, yet it took Mr. MacDonald and another man to hold the cradle still.

Objects around the apparently possessed house began to levitate, and the bullets and stones continued to fly in from outside and, when they were thrown into the river, they immediately reappeared on the property. The entity even began to torment the MacDonalds' dog.

News of the plague had spread far and wide. Mr. MacDonald especially was extremely unhappy about the extra attention, but the spirit seemed to thrive on the apparent recognition of its powers. It began to light small, spontaneous fires throughout the house. Each time flames flared up, they were beaten out—until the day that dozens of fires burst out all around the house at the same time. There was nothing the family could do except flee their once-peaceful home.

Devastated, the family moved in with relatives, but the spirit quickly found them and continued its evil in the temporary refuge. The MacDonalds moved again and, for a few days, they found the peace and quiet they had once taken for granted.

Then a mysterious black dog—or, more correctly, an apparition of a black dog—appeared on their hosts' doorstep. As mysteriously as it had appeared, the animal vanished, only to reappear, first on the roof of the house and then, at various times, in unlikely places. The spectre of the animal always disappeared after just a few moments. Its presence was widely believed to be responsible for the otherwise unexplainable deaths of animals owned by the MacDonalds.

The day that the house in which the MacDonalds were billeted rose up a metre from its foundation before setting itself back down again was the day that the beleaguered residents knew that the mysterious entity was completely out of control. The frightened folk called for help.

The first outsiders that they approached were the Natives who lived in surrounding encampments. The aboriginals were inclined to think that the family's suffering had not been caused by a ghost but by a witch who'd cast a spell on the household. They told the MacDonalds that the evil came from a southeasterly direction.

Next the family asked fellow settlers from nearby communities. These people shared the MacDonalds' cultural background, which included a belief in the paranormal. Because the sort of poltergeist-like activity that the family had endured is often associated with adolescent girls, the MacDonalds' foster daughter, Jane, was at first thought to have unwittingly caused the disturbances. So far, no one who had been consulted had been of any help.

Eventually the search for a satisfactory exorcism led the MacDonalds to a man known as Dr. John Troyer. What the man's degree might have been in has been lost through time, but it is chronicled that he was a mystic who had an even more psychically powerful daughter. She, it seemed, was gifted with second sight, having been the seventh born of a seventh born. The girl warned MacDonald that the torment he and his family had been exposed to had been caused by his enemy—an enemy who lived in a "long, low, log house."

John MacDonald recognized the description immediately. Just before all the trouble began, he had refused to sell a piece of property to a woman living in a "long, low, log house" located to the south and east of his land. Suddenly the horrible series of events began to make sense to him.

Troyer's daughter informed MacDonald that his life had been cursed by the angry woman, who occasionally took on the form of a grey goose to make her way onto his property. MacDonald acknowledged that he'd seen such a bird, and that it had a black head and dark feathers on its wings. The girl instructed the man to use a silver bullet to shoot the goose and then go directly to find the vengeful woman. If she were injured in the place where the bird was hit, then the MacDonalds would have the solution to their terrible mystery.

As soon as he was back home, MacDonald carried out the woman's instructions. The bullet he fired at the animal grazed its left wing. MacDonald stormed over to the woman's house and found her laid up, suffering from a very sore left arm. That retribution quieted most, but not all, of the supernatural activity.

The next unsettling event was first noticed by Jane, the MacDonalds' foster daughter. She arrived home ahead of the rest of her family, to find the family's furniture all stacked up along the perimeter of the inside of the house. The family Bible lay open and face down in the middle of this strange arrangement. The child ran to get John MacDonald and tell him what she'd seen. The man hurried into the house, made his way through the hedge of furniture and carefully picked up the Bible. He was hoping that something on the pages the book was open to would give him some kind of a clue about the force that had been meddling in his life for the past several years. Unfortunately, the Bible closed as soon as he lifted it. If there had been anything to be discerned from a specific passage on a specific page, he would never know.

Once again, the MacDonalds called upon the services of the mystical Dr. Troyer, who pronounced that if the possession did not cease at once, then the woman of the long, low, log house would have to be put to death. At this pronouncement, all signs of the haunting stopped and the MacDonalds lived out the balance of their lives in peace. The woman believed to have caused all the trouble also lived the rest of her days in the area, although as an outcast and with an injured arm.

Books and plays have been written about this nineteenth-century southwestern Ontario haunting, but there are still many unresolved issues surrounding it. The assumed perpetrator, the woman of the long, low, log house, is never once named or referred to in a way that would identify her any more specifically than that. This lack of information probably reflects the terrible intensity of the fear that the community felt of her, though she might only have been a victim herself—a victim of a witch-hunt in serious need of a villain. The Baldoon Mystery might well have been a classic case of a poltergeist haunting of an adolescent female.

As puzzling as the Baldoon Mystery is on its own, reports from that approximate area of the province some years later only increases the intrigue. The existence of these other stories lends great support to the theory that the paranormal disturbances in the MacDonald household were, in fact, caused by a poltergeist and not a curse.

In Crosshill, just north and west of Kitchener, George Manser, his wife and seven children were living in the farmhouse they'd built. It was the mid-1800s. Like the MacDonalds of Baldoon, the Mansers endured a three-year–long haunting that began quite suddenly. The similarities in the two chronicles are uncanny.

The first disturbance that the Mansers encountered was, coincidentally, with their windows—the panes of glass would suddenly shatter for no apparent reason. Mrs. Manser described the house as containing six windows and reported that four of the six broke and were replaced four times and the remaining two, twice. As in the earlier situation at Baldoon, it was impossible for vandals to have broken the windows without being observed. The breaks occurred during daytime, when anyone approaching the house could be easily seen. Eventually, like the MacDonalds in Baldoon, the beleaguered Manser family gave up replacing the glass and boarded up the windows.

Next the rains came—not unusual, you might think, except that these rains only occurred inside the Mansers' house. Time and time again, everything in their house—all their possessions—would be soaked with water. Despite intensive investigation by the family members and others, they were never able to determine a source for the sudden showers. Although some of the Manser children were adults at the time of this strange possession, others were still adolescents, so it is likely that the Mansers, like the MacDonalds before them, were experiencing a poltergeist haunting.

After three years of these supernatural disturbances, George Manser tore the old place down and built a new house. There is no record as to whether they were ever bothered by spontaneously shattering glass or indoor showers after moving to their replacement home.

During the time of the Manser haunting, a similar situation existed near Beaverton on the shores of Lake Simcoe. It seems Mr. and Mrs. Robert Dawson had just adopted a fourteen-year-old daughter. The child barely had time to settle into her new surroundings when spontaneous fires began to pop up throughout the Dawsons' house. The blazes were uncontrollable and reported to be unusually hot. The flames would burst out from a particular object in the home each time, and they were resistant to all attempts to extinguish them until whatever was burning was moved out of the house. Once outside, the flames quickly died away.

Like the MacDonalds, the Dawsons had no idea what they were dealing with, but obviously they did not have the readily available scapegoat equivalent to the woman of the long, low, log house. Instead, the Dawsons dealt with the evil presence that had invaded their home by sending their newly adopted daughter back to the orphanage.

Another haunting was taking place at roughly the same time as the Dawsons', but in the Chatham area, quite close to where Baldoon had once been. The similarities among these stories continue to increase, leaving any ghost hunter with a decidedly eerie feeling.

Little Lettie was thirteen years old in 1894 when the disturbances began. She'd been living calmly and happily with Mr. and Mrs. McDowell on their farm since they had adopted her when she was seven. That domestic bliss was permanently shattered during the late spring of 1894.

Afterwards, Mr. McDowell recalled for a newspaper reporter from the Toronto *Globe* that "...tobacco worms seemed to be gathering around the house from all quarters and made their way everywhere. One day my wife was washing in the cookhouse, when many of the disgusting things fell from the roof on[to] her back and all over her. These worms, which came by [the] hundreds, never touched anyone but my wife and, after a visit of nearly a month, [they] left as they had arrived, going in a body down the road."

McDowell continued, "Soon afterwards, myriads of red ants came up the concession and, arriving at the house, came in and made an extended stay. These also would bite my wife most unmercifully and not touch either myself or Lettie. I took [my wife] away for awhile and, during the time she was away, she was not bitten, but the moment she came home the ants met her at the gate. I then took her to a doctor, but he could make nothing of her case....After the ants,...crickets came in most unusual numbers and they, like the others, appeared to have [a] special liking for my wife."

It is a safe bet that a present-day explanation for those infestations would have attributed them to an adolescent girl directing subconscious angry energies at her adoptive mother.

The unseen forces at work in the McDowell household had, even after the last of these infestations, only begun to demonstrate themselves. By summer, sounds similar to the phantom footsteps of the Baldoon Mystery began to be heard through the McDowells' farmhouse. The footsteps were followed, at the end of September 1894, by a single stone mysteriously falling onto the cover of the family's rain barrel. No one could figure out where the goose-egg–sized rock may have come from but, before the family had time to give the matter much thought, a storm of gravel began to fly into the house through an open door.

Lettie ran to the field where her father was ploughing. By the time the child and the man made their way to the house, large stones were being propelled through the house windows, breaking the glass. Perhaps not knowing what he could do that would have helped, Mr. McDowell left the house once again to finish his chores. He had no sooner left than "nearly a bushel of gravel" poured into the house, Mrs. McDowell reported. She ran to bring her husband back, leaving Lettie alone with the supernatural force in the house. As soon as she was alone, a strange animal appeared to the girl. In an article in the Toronto *Globe* on September 26, 1894, Lettie described the phantom she saw initially as being "about three feet long, with a head like a cat and the same kind of whiskers as that animal...with claws...." The article also noted that "it growled at her."

Not long after that incident, Mrs. McDowell was also witness to the same animal apparition. When the apparition appeared to Lettie for a second time, the child told the reporter, "The animal

[that] came to the screen and tore it was the most terrible looking thing I ever saw. It was over two feet and a half feet with rough, shaggy, brown fur, a face somewhat like that of a man, but entirely covered with hair; it had long whiskers and ears like those of a cat. A short bushy tail completed the picture. It had its head through a hole it had ripped in the screen."

The strength of the haunting was intensifying. The family frequently heard heavy knocking at the front door. When they attempted to answer the knocks, there was no one there.

The stones began to rain down upon outbuildings around the property. Whatever was causing the possession no longer just directed its ire toward the family. Neighbours, concerned about what they'd heard was happening at the McDowell household, came to pay their respects and were treated to a veritable supernatural fiesta of poltergeist-like antics.

An old-timer in the area got wind of the strange events. He related a bit of local history to the McDowells that might— or might not—have accurately explained the source of the ghostly activity: "...when I was a young man...just about where Joe McDowell's little house now stands, [there was] a small deserted and tumbledown log hut, which...no one would pass after night. [T]he 'haunted hut,' folks called it."

The informant confided that at first he hadn't believed the scary stories that people told about the deserted shack. One day, however, his curiosity apparently got the best of him. He decided to see for himself what all the fuss was about.

"When I arrived near the hut, the very atmosphere seemed stifling and peculiarly oppressive and yet, I was not afraid but pushed on until I arrived just about where the present haunted house now stands. [There] I met a man dressed in plain, badly worn clothes going [in] the opposite direction. When I was nearly up to him...I put out my hand to shake hands with him and congratulate him on his pluck. He took my hand in his, when to my horror, I discovered I held the hand of a skeleton and then I saw that the head of the one whose hand I held was only a fleshless skull, the stare of whose empty sockets seemed to fairly freeze the very marrow in my bones. At the very moment I took its hand, the bush on every side seemed full of grinning skeleton-faces [that] glared at me from behind every tree and filled the air with hideous, discordant laughter. Then fine gravel began to rain down upon me, after which came stones of increasing size [that] beat me to the ground insensible. When I recovered conscious-ness, I was lying on a lounge in my own house. [My rescuers] told me they had found me lying on the cow-path through the bush. I never told the story to anyone till today. Nor did I ever go near that spot again after nightfall."

If the incident that the old man related was the truth, then it is no wonder that he never again approached the property after dark. There is also not much question as to the reason that the McDowells were suddenly dealing with unseen malevolent forces. It is equally possible, however, that the old man concocted the story to ease the community's current distress and that, in fact, the house was haunted by an especially active poltergeist that had attached itself to Lettie McDowell's adoles-cent energies.

The following story ran on June 18, 1901, in the newspaper Toronto *World*. The main headline, which was written all in capital letters, read "WHO THROWS THE STONES?" Under-neath there were three subheadings, the second of which was also all in capitals. These read, "House of a Man Living Near Perth Has Been Battered in a Lively Fashion," "TWENTY MEN CAN'T FIND THROWER" and finally, "Fusillade Occurs Between Eight and Ten O'Clock Every Night—Missiles Not Pebbles."

The body of the article was the following lengthy paragraph:

A traveler who visited Dalhousie this week tells of a remarkable occurrence—or a series of them—that has created much wonder and indignation in the locality. The dwelling of Mr. Scott, near the foot of Dalhousie Lake, has sustained a regular bombardment of stones for some days past, so that now there is scarcely a window pane left whole in the house. The fusillade began on the roof, and it was followed up by the missiles going thru [sic] the windows and striking other parts of the building, and it is said that some of the stones are as large as a man's fist. The house is not near the woods, [and] still no one has been seen doing the mischief, tho [sic] as many as 20 men have been on the watch. The occurrence takes place principall[y] at night, from 8 to 10 o'clock tho [sic], we are told, the stones have been thrown in the daytime as well. The throwing of such large stones so great a distance is a mysterious part of it and another strange thing is why such a thing should be done at all. Mr. Scott is a quiet, inoffensive man, and has given no reason why anyone should annoy him in such an alarming and dangerous manner. The neighbors are very sympathetic and are trying to assist in getting at the bottom of the outrage. Such occurrences have taken place in this locality. One happened in Perth many years ago and more recently one in the vicinity of Smiths Falls created the utmost wonder and apprehension for some time.

The article closed with a clear indication of the writer's skeptical opinion: "Of course, the outrage is the work of human agency and the perpetrator may be found out any time."

Or, given the history of this type of haunting in southern Ontario during the nineteenth century, perhaps the phrase should have been "the 'scapegoat' may be found any time."

The last ghost story in this chain of strikingly similar tales also occurred in the area of Perth, but considerably more recently—in 1935.

The Burgess family had recently moved to the area from their native Detroit. Signs of the haunting at their house began between Christmas and New Year's with an event that has now become an eerily familiar component of this chapter—stones being propelled through the windows of a farmhouse by some invisible force.

This more recent edition of a haunting began when a mirror mysteriously shattered, although no one visible was near it. Dishes were then thrown about the house, causing Mr. and Mrs. Burgess to be concerned for their children's welfare.

As with the previous stories, neighbours, along with local authorities, gathered to try to help solve the mystery. One visitor suggested that Mrs. Burgess and her older son, Michael, might have been behind the mischief in an attempt to get Mr. Burgess to take them out of the Canadian countryside and back to their urban American home.

An explanation for how the woman and the little boy, in additional incidents, would have been able to cause pieces of logs to levitate from the woodbox, or a long beef bone to travel through the air time and time again, was not offered. The signs of a serious haunting continued.

A heavy tool that Mr. Burgess had hung by a nail on a wall was seen to spin repeatedly, and three irons "walked" slowly down a staircase as a group of people who had gathered in the haunted house watched in terrified amazement.

Despite a thorough investigation by the Ontario Provincial Police and reporters for several daily newspapers, no reasonable explanation could ever be found for the ghostly disturbances. The Burgesses soon gave up their newly purchased haunted house and fled the area.

There are no doubt that more Ontario ghost stories that share characteristics with these ones, but even they considerably lessen the credibility of the theory that the Baldoon Mystery was caused by a curse, not a haunting.

Artifacts and Entities

No one's quite sure who the ghost at the Bytown Museum might have been when he was alive. Not surprisingly, as the building that houses the museum was built in 1827 and is the oldest stone building in the Ottawa area, it is home to at least one ghost.

"We do feel things," curator Lana Shaw explained during the filming of a local documentary show about hauntings.

Assistant curator Chantal Duport recalled starting work early one morning and hearing someone coming into the building, climbing up the stairs and entering the office area. As she was expecting her co-worker at about that time, she was not at all startled by the sounds—until she turned around to say good morning and found she was alone in the room. Further investigation revealed that she was alone in the building. The co-worker that she had been expecting did not arrive for another fifteen minutes.

That incident couldn't have been entirely surprisingly to Chantal, because the ghostly activity in the building has even had the fire department curious. The smoke detectors, which are scattered in strategic locations throughout the building, are protected by plastic covers. Once, all ten covers dropped to the floor in unison.

Considering the building's long and illustrious history, it is no wonder that the Bytown Museum is home to a ghost.

The Museum of Nature in Ottawa is also haunted. Doors will open and close on their own, and apparently sourceless shadows are occasionally seen in the building's hallways. A security guard reported that he had felt an icy hand being laid on his shoulder when there was no one—no one visible, that is—near him.

One day a worker trying to get the floors clean became extremely frustrated when the cord to her vacuum cleaner would not stay plugged into the electrical outlet. Although the cord was not pulled taut at any time, as soon as she moved around a corner, the plug would come out of its socket, as though it had been yanked out by some unseen hand.

Not surprisingly, when Ottawa film producer Alice d'Anjou and her colleague Shannon Fisher were in the initial stages of shooting a documentary about local hauntings, she reported, "I had a very 'chilled' feeling in the corridor where the cleaner had so much trouble with her electrical plug."

Alice added that there have also been "some reports of a slim, tall, dark man in a dark suit with piercing eyes appearing on the fourth-floor balcony looking onto the main atrium. Oddly, when I was standing in the atrium…discussing these hauntings, I was just letting my eyes roam across the space, 'scouting' for shots. I kept coming back to one corner on one of the upper levels, thinking it would be a great 'up shot' to pan across to set the mood." Later, while touring the place, Alice realized that the spot she'd felt so drawn to was the one where the apparition had been reported.

There are many theories as to who might be haunting the Museum of Nature. Some people feel it might be the spirit of Sir Wilfrid Laurier, who lay in state there for a while after his death in 1919. More likely, it is that of the building's architect, who killed himself by jumping from the roof of the building. Another theory is that it is the ghost of the Cree warrior whose costume is on display in the museum.

There is at least one other ghost story associated with the history of the museum itself. "Early reports of hauntings at the museum used to centre on Egyptian mummies stored in the dark labyrinths of [the] storage areas in the basement," d'Anjou hinted.

Considering all that has transpired in the old building over the years, it's not surprising that there is evidence of ghostly habitation.

Another museum included in Alice and Shannon's production is the Victoria School Museum in Carleton Place. Alice explained, "The strangest experience we had shooting this show was here. Our original visit was on a sunny afternoon and nothing seemed amiss. Shannon and Mike [another member of the production crew] returned a few weeks later to film. It was a cold, drizzly night and they arrived about twenty minutes early. They saw lights on in the second-floor windows. Thinking the curator, whom they were supposed to meet, might be there working and waiting for them, they tried the front door, which was unlocked. There were no lights [lit] on the ground floor and no one answered their calls. Thinking, gee, this was nice of him to leave it open for us on such an awful night, Mike and Shannon just found some light switches and started to get set up, grateful that they could start early and get in from the cold.

"The curator arrived about half an hour later, asking how they had gotten in. He swore he had locked the door earlier that day when he left," Alice explained. The pair must have been quite unnerved at this point but the worst was yet to come. The curator took them upstairs to show them the second floor where, on their arrival they'd noted there were lights shining.

"The second floor is now [used for] storage [of] artifacts and the windows are all boarded up and painted black to protect the artifacts from sunlight," Alice related

Clearly there was no way that they could have seen light coming through those windows—but they had. And Shannon and Mike are not the only ones to have seen strange things in those windows. Chris Gangel, the museum curator, told the production team that people living in neighbouring houses will avoid walking around the building after dark. They find it unnerving to see apparitions at the boarded-up second-storey windows when such sights should be impossible.

In Ottawa at least, it would seem that you don't have to be a "culture vulture" to haunt a museum.

Prime Minister Brought Spirit to Ottawa

Politicians aren't usually at the top of the list of people we consider likely to be psychically sensitive but, oddly, one of the most apparently uninteresting of our federal leaders was actually an active spiritualist. I refer, of course, to former Prime Minister William Lyon Mackenzie King. For the purposes of this book specifically, it's intriguing to note that King's grandfather—the first mayor of Toronto, William Lyon Mackenzie—has also left behind a supernatural legacy (see "Is It—or Isn't It—Haunted?" on p. 186).

Mackenzie King began to contact spirits of the dead regularly from 1932 to 1935, a period when he was Leader of the Opposition and therefore had considerably more time than when he was prime minister. King and Joan Patteson, his long-time friend and former next-door neighbour, became all but obsessed with the paranormal phenomenon of contacting spirits.

Much of this supernatural activity was conducted in King's home, a mansion left to him by the widow of his political mentor—and another former prime minister—Wilfrid Laurier. King named the place "Laurier House," and it was here that he and Joan developed a communication system to contact those "beyond the veil." They used a piece of furniture that King always referred to as the "little table" and they talked to dozens and dozens of historical figures, as well as seeking advice and comfort from Isabelle King, the prime minister's much-loved mother.

The pair obviously enjoyed these seances despite the time-consuming sessions, which must have been trying on the participants' patience. King and Patteson had created a code whereby a leg of the little table would tap out messages from the entities. One tap meant the letter "A," two taps the letter "B" and so on. Judging from the success of their seances, it is no wonder that the two enjoyed being in the presence of spirits at least as much being in the company of the living. Spirits from all periods in history visited Laurier House over the years when King was most actively involved in contacting the dead.

King's legacy of spiritualism has apparently lived on in the house, which is now a public museum. While researching a documentary for Halloween viewing, Ottawa-based film producers Alice d'Anjou and Shannon Fisher spoke with staff at Laurier House. They learned that King's third-floor study has been re-created to look as it did during the man's residency in the house. This re-creation includes a veritable shrine that the prime minister had arranged as a tribute to his deceased mother. King always left the lamp nearest this important area turned on. To be historically accurate, during the daytime when there are visitors, that same lamp is still left turned on. At night when the security staff locks up, they turn it off. But keeping the lamp turned off can be a problem. One guard spoke of turning the switch off and making his way down the stairs. When he got to the main floor, he heard a *click* from upstairs. He went back up and found the bulb in the lamp burning brightly. He turned it off, went back downstairs and once again heard the light being switched on. He went back up to the study and found that the lamp had mysteriously been turned on once again.

That guard is not the only one to have noted the lamp being lit when it shouldn't have been. Neighbours in surrounding homes have reported that there was a light shining through a third-floor window when they knew that Laurier House was locked and empty. Some people have felt paranormal presences so strongly that they have refused to work in Laurier House. They've said that even though they've known that they were alone, they've felt that there was someone there with them and that feeling was strong enough to make them choose to stay away.

The other house that King caused to become haunted was his vacation property across the river in the province of Quebec. Not only did he encourage ghosts to visit there when he was alive but, since his death, William Lyon Mackenzie King's own image has been seen haunting the Kingsmere estate on numerous occasions.

Chapter **5**

CLASSIC ONTARIO GHOST STORIES

Philip, the Carefully Constructed Phantom

The "Philip Experiment" took place in Toronto in the early 1970s. It eventually captured international attention and it's no wonder. The "Group of Eight," as the participants called themselves, had accomplished ground-breaking paranormal research. They had manifested a ghost.

The experiment began after members of the Toronto Psychic Society had been called in to investigate a haunted house. The investigators had been told of a suicide in the house but, when they viewed a hanging apparition, they wondered if their own expectations had not played an important role in the sighting. They decided to see if they could create an entity where none had previously existed.

Toward this end, one member of the group was assigned to create an entirely fictitious personality and place him in an era and a place. This, then, was the conception of Philip. It was decided that he would have been an aristocratic Englishman in the mid-1600s who lived a tragic life. Although married to one woman, he was in love with another. Philip's wife had the mistress executed and Philip, unable to live without her, eventually killed himself.

The Group of Eight met regularly and meditated together in the hope that their manifestation would appear. To some degree they patterned their experiment after Victorian seances in that they had placed a small table in their midst through which they hoped the ghost would communicate. Unlike many other seances, however, they made sure that their meetings were always held in well-lit rooms and that an observer was always present. None of those involved wanted to be tricked by any sort of a sham. The person assigned to observe the sessions noted that, for more than a year, the only result that the group procured was that all of those present had readily discernible auras while they meditated.

Understandably discouraged with the lack of results, the group discussed alterations to their original plan. It was decided that rather than solely concentrating on manifesting Philip, they would engage in light conversation with one another while still keeping their actual purpose in mind. That change, it seemed, marked the turning point and Philip, as an active presence, was born after just a few of those less intense sessions.

The first clue that something supernatural was in their midst was evident, as they had hoped, through the table. At first the table gave off mild vibrations but, after awhile, it began to actually move. Although clearly delighted to finally have their patience rewarded, the participants didn't, initially, know what to make of the change and how best to deal with it. Soon, however, a plan that included a code for communication was introduced. The group would verbally acknowledge Philip's presence and then put forth questions that required "yes" or "no" answers only. One knock of the table would be a positive reply; two, a negative one.

After just a very few sessions, something uncanny happened. The table developed a distinctive personality of its own. When it was happy, it would reply enthusiastically, moving energetically all around the room. When it didn't want to answer a question, there were scratching sounds. If it wasn't sure of an answer, it would reply with a decidedly hesitant series of knocks.

The group was fascinated and everyone attended every meeting they could. Inevitably, however, there were evenings when one or more of the Group of Eight found it necessary to be absent for one reason or another. Interestingly, Philip and/or the table's personality changed as the composition of the group changed. Occasionally Philip's antics were not simply confined to the table. He would turn lights on and off and move things about.

It didn't take long for the press to get wind of the experiment. The CBC sent a television crew in to investigate for the public affairs program *Man Alive*. "Mary," a participant in the group who agreed to share her recollections of the events as long as she was guaranteed anonymity, recalled, "We had a really fun time with the cameramen as they could not keep up with where the table was going. We never seemed to have control of which direction the table went."

Of course, once the word was out, the group was in demand on the talk-show "circuit" of the day.

Mary described, "Other times we were filmed in the studios. I remember one [such incident] in particular because we were not getting much response from the table. The MC was making disparaging remarks about our lack of success. I think that was all [that the situation] needed because we said, 'Go get him Philip' and the table chased him right up a few stairs to where he was going to sit. That made us all laugh so hard that we had no more problems with getting responses as we needed them."

Even some of the academic community became interested in the Philip Experiment. The participants and the table were flown to Kent State University. Some of the scholars were interested in measuring the actual physical force that the participants' group creation exerted.

"At one point we had the table with only one leg off the floor. The people testing us could not get the leg back down no matter how much force was used," Mary recalled, before adding with a chuckle, "One man was dead set against what was going on and he was bound and determined to be a negative influence on everybody. But we were hyped up to such a point that we could override him. At the end of an evening we said to the table, 'Go get him Philip' and you've got PhDs and goodness knows what else, running all down this hallway trying to stay clear of Philip. It was so funny to look at. All these professors with a table running after them. It only went from bad to worse, the darned table was climbing the stairs. It was really strong. Altogether... it was a very interesting weekend."

Amusing anecdotes aside, the Philip episodes are as interesting now as they were twenty-five years ago. Just what was at work? Mary suggested that, "as a group we had somehow been able to telepathically communicate what we wanted to happen," which led back full circle to the original haunted house investigation that was the impetus for conducting the experiment.

All these years later Mary is still grateful that she had the opportunity to be part of such an experiment.

"In retrospect it was exciting to have been involved but at the time it was fun. You didn't think of it in terms of any kind of ground breaking until we started getting invitations to the television stations and the book came out. It hit the parapsychologists hard. Then we realized we had done something that nobody else had done but at the time it seemed like just sheer utter nonsense. I think if we had taken ourselves too seriously it would never have happened. We never thought of it in terms of going anywhere outside the group," Mary explained.

On a more personal level, her involvement helped Mary considerably at the time and actually made permanent changes in some of her attitudes.

"For me the most I got out of this [participation] was the [sense of the] overwhelming power of what the mind can do. If nothing else was learned I learned to believe in my own mental ability, not just as part of the Philip group but with anything I had to do. I feel that there is little I cannot accomplish if I really want to. I do not necessarily accomplish very much but whatever I do, I know that it is only my own mind that either stops me or forces me on," Mary assessed. "I don't know about anybody else but I knew that my mind was helping to control that table, therefore if I can do that there is nothing to stop me except my own mind. I feel my involvement has affected the entire rest of my life. Oh, I believe wholeheartedly."

For the ghost of a man who never really existed, Philip's impact was certainly profound and long lasting.

The Angel Inn

In January 1998 I received a beautifully scripted note from the current owner of the Angel Inn, Niagara-on-the-Lake. Peter Ling wrote in response to my inquiry about the inn's long-standing status as a haunted building. He began his kind letter by saying that he had taken over the hotel and that Florence Ledoux, the former owner, had died. This sad news immediately made me wonder whether the resident ghost, Captain Colin Swayze, might now have gone on to other haunts. Ling's second sentence, however, relieved me of my concerns.

"Captain Swayze still makes himself known to us from time to time," he reported. That was indeed good news for all of us who enjoy a ghost story with a long and colourful history.

Buildings situated on the land that we now identify as 224 Regent Street, Niagara-on-the-Lake, have welcomed guests since the 1700s, when the Harmonious Coach House first opened its doors. While the history of the haunting does not go that far back, it is an extremely old ghost story by Canadian standards.

Captain Swayze was a British officer during the War of 1812. A year after the war began, Swayze was captured by American troops who incarcerated, tortured and eventually killed him in the log cabin that was the forerunner to the building that houses today's Angel Inn. His soul has roamed the property ever since.

The ghost's identity first came to light some five generations ago when the captain apparently introduced himself to the man who owned the inn at that time. After a psychic confirmed the other-worldly information, the Angel Inn's owners initiated a search for genealogical information from England. Their efforts were rewarded, not only with the information they requested, but also with a painting of their resident ghost. The latter established the long-deceased man as an important part of the Angel Inn household and, of course, he is still a focal point at the hotel.

Swayze's descendants in England explained that the captain had been a talented man. He was both musical and artistic. He must also have been of a generous nature, for Florence

Ledoux always credited his ghostly instruction with her own ability to play the piano, sculpt and draw.

The haunting is such a strong one that periodically people sense the very essence of the era from which the ghost originates. Vague apparitions of nineteenth-century soldiers, as well as ghostly military music from that era, have been perceived in different rooms of the Angel Inn. Fortunately, most of the hotel's overnight guests appreciate that the inn is haunted—otherwise the sight of a slightly see-through man wearing a red jacket would undoubtedly come as something of a shock.

Swayze clearly feels that he has something of a proprietary interest in the inn. Perhaps that is why he reacts so vigorously to confrontations. The spirit has been known to become agitated when management and a member of the staff at the inn were arguing. He made his displeasure known by causing dishes and cups to be strewn about the room in which the two were trying to work out their differences.

Judging by Peter Ling's experience, Captain Swayze has not changed much over the years. He certainly still likes to get introductions out of the way early on in a relationship.

Ling explained it to me this way, "...shortly after we purchased the inn from Mrs. Ledoux I was staying overnight in the oldest part of the inn, all alone. It was a cold and stormy night with no moon. I was awakened around 3 a.m. by a terrible crash! Upon investigation I eventually discovered that a large iron horseshoe that I had brought to the inn for good luck and which had been nailed above the fireplace had been wrenched from the wall and hurled across the room where it ended up facing the inn door. All the doors and windows were locked. In the morning when I retrieved the horseshoe there on the inn's step was a copy of the local *Niagara Advance* newspaper. The headline read, 'New Owner of Angel Inn Wants to Meet Capt. Swayze.'"

Ling, apparently a master of understatement, closed his correspondence to me this way: "I considered myself introduced."

Hockey Hauntings

Given that hockey is Canada's national sport, it's only fitting that our folklore heritage should include a sprinkling of supernatural hockey stories—and it does.

The Hockey Hall of Fame is located inside a 150-year-old Bank of Montreal building that has been incorporated into the interior of a modern office tower in downtown Toronto. The juxtaposition of the old architecture inside the new is undeniably eye-catching, but it is also functional in that it protects the aging facade from any possible damage by exposure. By happiest coincidence this arrangement has also preserved the home of at least one ghost.

Dorothy's spirit has haunted the old Bank of Montreal building since the early 1950s. Dorothy worked as a teller in the building. The most frequently told story goes that she was involved in a relationship with a man who also worked at the bank. Some renditions of the story declare he was the bank manager, while others maintain he was a fellow teller. A third and considerably more fanciful version of the tale has her involved with members of the Irish Republican Army who were planning to rob the bank and ship the money back to aid the cause in their homeland. This last rendition lacks credibility on a number of levels, including one as basic as the woman's name. Records do confirm that the woman's name was Dorothy, not "Doreen," as is claimed in the more colourful but decidedly suspect telling.

Fortunately, none of that matters at all, as this is not a ghost story that requires any embellishment. The facts alone make it most intriguing, and those facts begin early one morning in March 1953.

Len Redwood, chief messenger for the bank, was already in the building around 7 a.m. It was his habit to arrive so early, but he was surprised when one of the tellers, Dorothy, showed up just a little while later. It must have been a pleasant surprise for Redwood, for Dorothy was considered one of the nicest people on staff. Redwood was quoted in 1983, thirty years after the incident, as saying she was "always smiling."

The man's surprise turned to concern when he realized that the young woman looked "pretty rough," like she'd had a tough night. He wasn't surprised, therefore, when she went straight into the women's washroom. After a considerable length of time, Dorothy emerged from the toilet facilities, went downstairs for a moment, and then returned to the washroom. Seconds later a shot rang out and Dorothy lay dead on the washroom floor. She had killed herself with a single shot to her head, using the standard bank-issue revolver. (In those days, banks kept firearms available for the staff. In case of a robbery they were expected to defend their employer's funds by shooting at anyone who tried to rob them.)

Signs of the haunting began almost immediately. Dorothy's female co-workers refused to use the upstairs washroom where the woman had killed herself. They all reported feeling distinctly uncomfortable in the room, and eventually the Bank of Montreal gave in and built new toilet facilities in the basement.

That expense didn't provide complete protection from an awareness of Dorothy's presence, however. Staff knew, when

Dorothy's ghost roams the halls of the Hockey Hall of Fame, apparently unaware that the building is no longer the bank in which she was employed during her lifetime.

lights came on by themselves and securely locked doors were found open, that Dorothy's spirit lingered on. Even as recently as the 1980s, messenger Redwood spoke to the press about generally accepted feelings among the staff that they were being watched when no one visible was in the room. Items that the bank employees required in their daily duties would often go missing for a period of time, only to turn up later, just as mysteriously, at an unexpected place.

The custodial staff were perhaps the most severely affected. As they worked away in the dark and quiet of night, they frequently reported hearing unexplainable sounds, some as distressing as shrieking and moaning.

Being abandoned as a Bank of Montreal branch and then becoming the home of the Hockey Hall of Fame has not changed the former bank's status as a haunted building.

Christine Simpson, in charge of public relations for the Hall of Fame at the time of its opening, made reference to the ghost story during a preview tour group that she was escorting through the facility. One woman in the group apparently "looked frantic" upon hearing this news because she had distinctly felt an invisible presence only moments before.

At about that time, as well, two employees with the Hall of Fame were working late into the evening to complete everything that needed to be done for the museum's official opening. When they finally decided to leave for the night, one employee asked the other what he or she had been doing going up and down the stairs so often.

"What do you mean, what was I doing?" came the reply. "What were you doing? I was at my desk the whole time."

The incorrect presumption that it was their colleague they were hearing wandering around the building had provided both of them with peace of mind while they completed their chores. Conversely, regardless whether Dorothy continues to move items around in the former bank building or not, she's occasionally but good-naturedly blamed for such mischief if an employee misplaces something.

Perhaps the most dramatic recent proof of Dorothy's continuing presence in the building where she worked and loved, and later died, was the reaction of a small boy touring the Hockey Hall of Fame in 1995. Kelly Masse, currently responsible for public information there, described the incident this way. The child was with adults and all were enjoying touring the exhibits when, for no reason that the adults in the group could see, the child stopped in his tracks. His unusual and sudden stance was noted by those with him and they asked the child what was wrong. He pointed off into what appeared to the others to be empty space. When questioned further he exclaimed over and over, "Can't you see it? Can't you see it?" When he realized that no, in fact, the adults with him could not see what he was seeing, he described the image. "He described her [Dorothy] perfectly," acknowledged Kelly Masse.

This incident provides proof that Dorothy, the tragically jilted bank teller, lives on amid Canada's tributes to our country's hockey heroes.

The following story is one of the most intriguing hockey legends ever to come out of Ontario, but is there a paranormal link? You be the judge.

The place—Maple Leaf Gardens

The date—April 21, 1951

The moment—2:53 into sudden-death overtime in the fifth and potentially deciding game for the Stanley Cup. The Toronto Maple Leafs were home to the Montreal Canadiens. The series had been a see-saw battle so far, each game decided by a single, overtime goal. This one would be no exception.

The hero—an unlikely one only in that Bill Barilko was a Leaf defenceman—a valued player but clearly not one the team usually counted on for his scoring abilities. On this night, however, those were exactly the skills that earned his team the ultimate reward in hockey—Lord Stanley's cup.

The boisterous celebrations of Barilko's goal began on-ice and continued off-ice and long into the night. Twenty-four-year-old Barilko was a hero among heroes and for days he stayed around Toronto, close to his teammates, enjoying the glory. Weeks later, after the hoopla had simmered down, young Bill decided to escape from the city for awhile and indulge in one of his other passions—fishing—on one of northern Ontario's well-stocked lakes.

He never made it. Bill Barilko, hockey's newest hero, an athlete in peak form who should have had at least another fifty good years of life ahead of him, was, as was later discovered, dead—killed instantly when the plane taking him to a remote fishing spot crashed into a heavily forested, isolated location.

Spring turned to summer, the leaves on the trees in the Ontario forest grew fuller and denser, hiding the crash site even more effectively. That fall, the Maple Leaf's training camp began with an eerie emptiness. Bill Barilko's usual spot in the dressing room stood vacant. The other players' friend and the fans' hero had not yet been found.

As professional athletes, the team members set aside their concern and, to the best of their abilities, went about trying to follow their missing comrade's example. These hockey players needed to do what they were being paid to do—win hockey games. And they did win a few. But, when it came to stringing together a series of wins, or coming out on top of the important games, the Maple Leafs consistently fell short. The Stanley Cup champions fared poorly, not only that year but for the next eleven years. It seemed as though the team was jinxed.

Coincidentally, Bill Barilko's remains lay undiscovered through the four changing seasons of each of those eleven years. Only the most sensitive soul examining the situation might have connected the two circumstances.

By the 1961–62 season, the Toronto Maple Leafs had finally begun to resemble the powerhouse team they were more than a decade before. The players united to fight their way through the season and on to the finals.

In May 1962, the wreckage of the plane containing Bill Barilko's body was spotted. At last the hero could be brought home for a proper, respectful burial—just days after the Toronto Maple Leafs finally won the Stanley Cup once again.

Could Barilko's restless spirit have been responsible for the long dry spell as well as the eventual win? There are some people, including the Canadian rock group Tragically Hip, who think so. Their song "Fifty Mission Hat" is, in part, a tribute to the apparent mysterious and possibly paranormal correlation between one man's disappearance and a hockey team's success. Listen for Bill Barilko's name the next time you hear the song.

Ghosts of The Grange

The ghosts of The Grange in Toronto are among the most accepted in Ontario. Of course, any building with as much history as that one would be sadly lacking if it were not haunted. The elegant old residence was built in 1817 on an enormous parcel of land. By 1911, its lot size had dwindled considerably and the home had become a public art gallery. It had also become haunted.

Security guards at the Art Gallery of Ontario have given sketchy reports of seeing phantom lights dart about the place. There have also been very detailed reports of actual apparitions appearing for sufficient lengths of time that frightened witnesses were able to give detailed accounts of what they had seen.

More recently, however, a cleaner assigned to a shift when The Grange was not open to the public was working away at her duties blissfully unaware that she was not as alone as she'd thought she was. About to make the routine climb to the second floor, the woman looked up to the top of the staircase. There, at the top of the stairs, staring down at her, stood a man.

Although the image made no move to approach her, the sight of him alone was enough to terrify the woman. She fled from The Grange that very second and has never returned.

Volunteer Elayne Dobel's reported sighting shared some similarities with that of the frightened cleaner but was considerably more detailed. She was closing the shutters in the drawing room one evening when a movement in the periphery of her vision caught her eye. There, in the room with her, was a man in a yellow velvet waistcoat. The image walked across the room and through a wall at a point where a doorway had once existed, and disappeared completely from sight.

There seems to be very little question that this one soul at least, who was once associated with The Grange, has not yet come to accept his own mortal demise.

A Grisly Ghost Story

"Queen's Park." In Ontario today, those words are synonymous with the seat of the province's parliament, but 150 years ago the land on which the legislative buildings now stand was occupied by an "insane asylum." The ghosts that roam the halls, tunnels and staircases of Queen's Park today are generally thought to be remnants from that original institution.

There seems to be little controversy about the imposing old building's status as a haunted house of parliament. Of course, given the number of ghostly sightings and the diversity of the people reporting those sightings, it really would be futile to adopt an official policy of denial. The ghosts are even noted in Claire Hoy's biography of long-time Ontario premier Bill Davis.

The most gruesome spectre is somewhat similar to one of the ghosts in the haunted Keg restaurant (see "Spirits with Your Meal?" on p. 202)—both are female apparitions who have hanged themselves. Two other female spirits are equally as clearly seen. One is dressed all in white and the other has her checked dress draped over her head.

The only man haunting Queen's Park is the manifestation of an old soldier. Although he too is clearly and frequently seen, no one has yet been able to identify the uniform he wears, which of course would reveal what era he lived in. If it were determined that he fought on the side of a losing cause, it might also explain the decidedly unpleasant look on that ghost's face. Or perhaps being doomed to an eternity of rubbing shoulders with politicians is sufficient cause to scowl.

The four ghosts at Queen's Park are among the oldest in the province and certainly the best known and most widely accepted.

Soldiering On

A small but significant paragraph appeared in the spring 1998 issue of Canada's history magazine, *The Beaver*. It reported that Lundy House, in Niagara Falls, dating to *circa* 1792, had been demolished the previous December. If this were not travesty enough, the short article added that the ground the historic stopping-off point had occupied for nearly two hundred years would now be home to a shopping mall. According to an area historian consulted at the time of the demolition, many of the onlookers wept.

Such an emotional reaction was no doubt well justified. There is little as painful to a history lover as watching a piece of the past disappear. It would have been even more interesting if there had been some way to record the reactions of the phantom soldiers as they passed by the house on their customary route.

Over the years, five apparitions, clad in uniforms from the War of 1812, have been seen frequently. They appear to have fought a hard battle and are slowly making their way back to safety. Witnesses' descriptions combined with historians' reports indicate that the men were likely soldiers killed in the Battle of Lundy's Lane. Although their mortal bodies are likely buried nearby, clearly their souls have not yet been put to rest.

The ghosts of soldiers who fought in the War of 1812 have been seen walking down Lundy's Lane where Lundy House stood for more than two hundred years.

The Haunted Hall

Toronto's "Old City Hall" has a lot in common with a similar edifice several provinces west, for the City of Calgary also has refurbished its original house of civic politics. Both buildings date back to the turn of the twentieth century, both were constructed of sandstone and both are home to ghosts (see *More Ghost Stories of Alberta*).

Given the colourful events that have taken place over the years in and around Toronto's proud old hall, it would be surprising only if the place were *not* haunted. Life at its happiest and its most tragic has been played out in this building. Right from its construction, drama has surrounded the stately old place. Architect Edward James Lennox asked that a plaque be placed on the building crediting him with the hall's design and construction. He was turned down and responded by creating his own cleverly surreptitious tribute. Lennox ingeniously immortalized his association with the building by carving one character at the top of every fourth exterior pillar. When those letters and numbers are read in sequence, they reveal the man's first initials, last name, his title of architect and the year the building was constructed.

John Shaw, the mayor of Toronto at the time the hall was completed, was not as willing to forego his moment in the sun. On a July morning in 1898 Mayor Shaw and his wife stood in a wooden bucket while it was hoisted up some 80 metres. From this rather precarious perch they ceremoniously laid the building's last stone.

Since that day, generations of Torontonians have played out some of their life dramas within its walls. The wedding chapel has hosted thousands and thousands of couples who have chosen to tie the knot more expediently than romantically. And then there are the courtrooms. Over the years infamous criminals, including the last two men to be sentenced to death in Canada, have been tried there.

It is in these courtrooms and on nearby staircases that most of the ghostly activity takes place—and there is a lot of it taking place. Judges accessing different floors via particular stairways will frequently hear footsteps beside them or feel their gowns being tugged, but a look around quickly assures the rather startled magistrates that they are alone. The footsteps are light, suggesting that the ghost is possibly the spirit of a woman or a child rather than a man. These phantom sounds have been heard so often by the judges that, by now, the invisible presences are simply an accepted part of working in the creaky old place.

A newspaper reporter who attempted to spend Halloween night in one of the courtrooms wasn't nearly so accepting. Although she'd taken her sister along for company and support, she didn't sleep a wink and both two young women fled before dawn. Mysteriously appearing misty vapours in the room and frightening sounds convinced them that whatever was there with them did not want them to stay. By 4 a.m. they had had quite enough and were more than willing to let the ghost or ghosts have the privacy they apparently wanted.

The northwest attic is another area believed to be haunted. Even hard-core skeptics become uncomfortable there. Occasionally, housekeeping and maintenance staff have gone so far as to refuse to work in certain areas of the haunted building. One night a cleaner stared in terror as dark figures appeared near the judge's bench in a deserted courtroom. The images watched the man intently before they disappeared as suddenly and mysteriously as they had appeared. Those particularly frightening manifestations may help to make up the figure of fifty that some say is the ghostly population in the old city hall. No wonder the place is considered to be one of the most haunted buildings in all of Canada.

Mind the Lady

Despite its majestic appearance, the building at 51 Stuart Street in Hamilton has served some decidedly pragmatic functions. Custom House, an imposing example of Victorian architecture, was built in 1860 to house the customs department. Since then, the building has served as an army recruiting centre, a flophouse, a macaroni factory and a martial arts academy. Today it houses the Ontario Workers Arts and Heritage Centre (OWAHC).

Throughout all of these changes, one fact has remained constant—the building is haunted. The first documented reference to the ghost appeared during 1873, in a poem written and published by Alexander Wingfield, then an employee at Custom House. No one knows for sure who the entity was when she was alive, but the "Black Lady," or "Dark Lady," as she is commonly known, is as much in residence today as she ever was.

In the 1940s, three girls attending Murray Street School, behind Custom House, reported seeing a slightly transparent figure of a beautiful woman in a top-floor window of the haunted customs building. They were so frightened by the sight that they were still unnerved in 1997 when they recounted the experience.

Civic official John Kenyon experienced a similar sighting in the 1970s when he was a boy. Like the girls so many years before, Kenyon was badly frightened by the sight of the apparition and never set foot inside the building again until 1997, and only then because it was important to his electoral success.

In 1988, when a martial arts academy occupied Custom House, a woman identified only as Annette reported "many unusual incidents," according to staff at the OWAHC. As these events included a disembodied male voice ordering her to "get out of here," it is likely that the Dark Lady is not alone in her eternity. Annette also noted cool and unexplained breezes, doors mysteriously opening when no one was near them and light switches and other electrical equipment that often seemed to be operated by an invisible hand. Perhaps the most bizarre and unsettling sight, though, was the sudden appearance of the image of a cat that was apparently caught between a storm window and an inside window—both of which had been nailed shut for months.

In 1996, when renovations were underway to adapt the place to its intended designation as the Ontario Workers Arts and Heritage Centre, the ghostly activity increased dramatically. Workers arriving in the morning occasionally found their tools scattered about even though when they'd left the night before everything had been put away. Once, rather than finding them lying about on the floor, they discovered that the ghost had stacked all the tools in a precarious, ceiling-high pile.

A painter, Jim MacDonald, not only saw but actually communicated with at least one of the ghosts. He was working alone one night when he sensed, more than saw, that he had invisible company. After a while, an image began to take shape— the image of a woman in her mid-80s, approximately 1.7 metres in height and all dressed in black. She warned the tradesman that if, during the renovations, a particular mantelpiece was

At Custom House, Hamilton's "Dark Lady" seems to be a permanent resident.

moved, a flood would occur. (Staff now believe that the Black Lady used to brush her long flowing hair in the mirror that hung above the mantel.) Despite the ghost's admonition, the mantelpiece was removed. Shortly afterward, every room in Custom House was flooded when a roof drain broke.

After the flooding incident, many of the people associated with Custom House began to take the presence very seriously. It was actually proposed that they communicate information about the planned renovations to the spirit via a clairvoyant, but the members of the board responsible for the changes voted down the suggestion.

Nevertheless, the Black Lady's further communications were heeded. When she somehow managed to communicate a dislike for a particular shade of paint, the colour choice was changed and the job was completed without further incident. Perhaps, like many people still alive, she is easy to please as long as she gets things her way.

At one point during the renovations, the word "murder" became visible on a wall in the northeastern room of the main floor. The only explanation to date is that the entity was attempting to communicate by way of some ghostly vandalism.

According to staff at the OWAHC, a woman who had visited Custom House experienced a very disturbing dream afterward. The dream, it is reported, "began as a rape scene in the basement of Custom House. The victim in the dream managed to escape through a tunnel in the foundation of the building, emerging on the [nearby] train tracks or the water's edge." The staff member elaborated that "[l]ater it was proposed that the dream may have freed a spirit trapped in the building."

Perhaps a spirit may have been released through that night terror, but later that same fall James Newbauer was serving his first-ever shift as a volunteer at the OWAHC. He shut the windows in what is now the main gallery and fastened the lock bars on the shutters. Seconds later, when James and employee Andrew DeNew rechecked those same windows, they found them unlocked.

The following year, two men were working in the gallery throughout the night in order to finish a display installation. One of the locks on one of the shutters that had given James trouble the previous year began to move back and forth, although no one was near it at the time, nor was there any breeze. One of the two installers, Steve Penefold, was quoted as saying, "It [the lock] kept swinging for an unnaturally long time."

Just a month after that incident, Mary Breen, the executive director of the OWAHC, chose to use the men's washroom while the women's was occupied by someone else. She learned, rather startlingly, that the Dark Lady doesn't approve of such egalitarian tactics. Alone in the room, Mary was washing her hands when the paper-towel dispenser flew off the wall where it was hung—with enough force that it hit the opposite wall before dropping to the floor.

Perhaps the strangest ghostly anecdote surrounding the legend of the Custom House ghost dates back to the era when the Naples Macaroni Company occupied the building (1956–79). The Reios, who owned the business, were well used to people who were once associated with the building paying a fond call to the old place. The most remarkable of those was a woman who introduced herself as the daughter of Alexander Wingfield, the customs agent who, in 1873, had written the poem about the ghost of Custom House.

The woman entertained Mr. and Mrs. Reio with recollections of times when she and her father had been in the basement of the old building and had seen a female image clad completely in black, who had disappeared and then reappeared. The visitor's stories scared Mrs. Reio so badly that it was years before she'd once again venture down to the cellar.

The Reios decided to check out the visitor's story through Hamilton resident Alex Wingfield, whose aunt was the daughter of the poet after whom he himself was named. At that point the Reios may have felt somewhat assured. Their assurance was quickly dashed, however, as he noted that his aunt had, in fact, moved to Vancouver. He explained further that to his knowledge his aunt had never returned to Ontario to visit and, furthermore, she had been dead for several years by the time of her reported visit to Custom House.

No explanation for the Reios' strange encounter has ever been offered.

Today, many of the people associated with Custom House enjoy that the building is haunted. The paranormal encounters have continued until the time of this writing and staff at the stately old building are assembling an exhibit recognizing the Dark Lady as an important facet in its heritage.

The Ghost of the Stonemason

There must have been a time, early in the year 1856, when Ivan Reznikoff considered himself to be the luckiest man in the entire world. He had recently arrived in Canada West from his native Russia. Offering only his skills as a stonemason, Reznikoff had immediately found work in the burgeoning young city of Toronto, where magnificent buildings were being constructed to house a university. He enjoyed not only his work but also the people he worked with, especially a fellow stonemason, a Greek named Paul Diabolos. Both men had been hired to create ornate granite gargoyles on the building that would become University College. Ivan and Paul got along so well working together that Ivan proudly introduced his fiancée, Susie, to his new colleague. That introduction heralded Ivan Reznikoff's demise and eventual reappearance on campus as a ghost.

It seems that Susie and Paul were quite attracted to one another and, although engaged to Reznikoff, the young woman began to see Diabolos as frequently as their schedules allowed. The Greek, who was apparently as diabolical as his last name might have implied, was not content just to steal Susie's affections. He began to carve a laughing gargoyle directly behind the one Reznikoff was working on. The imagery was clear—the Russian was being laughed at behind his back.

Suspicious that both his love life and his work life were collapsing around him, Ivan Reznikoff armed himself with an axe and a knife and set about spying on his beloved. When he spotted her sitting prettily on a bench with Diabolos, the Russian flew into a rage. He charged at the couple and chased his rival toward the door of the university tower. Sure that he had caught the scoundrel, Reznikoff swung his axe. Diabolos ducked and the blade lodged itself into a heavy oak door, which remains scarred to this day.

The two men pursued each other around the tower until Diabolos spotted Reznikoff's back. He hurled the cuckolded carver down the tower and to his death. The area was still under construction and Diabolos was easily able to bury the body—and with it the proof of his crime.

Having most effectively erased both his rival and his fatal deed, Paul Diabolos married the fair (if unfaithful) Susie and, we might presume, lived happily ever after. In fact, the couple might still have been living in wedded bliss when, on Valentine's Day in 1890, a man carrying a tray of kerosene lamps inside the university tower slipped and fell, igniting a fire that quickly devastated the building. During the clean-up process a mangled skeleton and a belt buckle were discovered. Although the workers probably didn't realize it at the time, they had just discovered Ivan Reznikoff's long-hidden body.

However, the discovery must have explained something to an academic named Falconbridge who, back in 1866, had reported seeing a ghost in the building. But unearthing Reznikoff's remains was apparently not enough to put his spirit to rest. During the late 1800s, student Alan Aylesworth, who went on to a most distinguished career that included being knighted, made a most astounding report about the ghost of Ivan Reznikoff. It seems that Aylesworth had been making his way across the campus one evening when he happened upon a heavy-set man. The two exchanged greetings that included comments on the severe cold that night. Aylesworth invited the stranger into his student residence and offered him a glass of spirits to help ward off the frigid temperatures.

Inevitably, the two fell into a conversation. The guest introduced himself by way of a tale—the details of his own murder.

The events that the strange man recounted were supported by physical proof around the university that the startled student had either seen or been told about over the years. There was, Aylesworth knew, a gouge out of the oak door to the tower. There were also photos in existence of the crew of stonemasons who'd created the bizarre ornaments around the campus buildings. The names of those artisans photographed included Ivan Reznikoff and Paul Diabolos.

After the guest had told his host the gruesome story that kept him from rest, he simply vanished. The only "proof" that Aylesworth could ever offer to support his story was the second, half-consumed glass of alcohol on his table and that even as a student he was not a man given to nonsense and certainly, as his career progressed, not a man who would have in anyway profited from having created such a yarn.

It would seem, therefore, that on that cold winter evening the man who went on to become an elected Canadian official, and eventually Sir Alan Aylesworth, shared a drink with the ghost of Ivan Reznikoff.

There have been sightings of Reznikoff since, although certainly none so dramatic as that one. If you visit the campus, you may not see the Russian stonemason's ghost but you can visit his eventual grave to the northeast of the tower where he was murdered. Curiously, his skull was never interred but was held in a University of Toronto administrator's office. The epitaph, "Rest in Peace," would be misplaced for this restless soul.

An Unsettled Spirit

Internationally renowned landscape artist Tom Thomson drowned under mysterious circumstances on July 8, 1917. His death at that time and in that manner was not only a great tragedy but a shock to all who knew him. Thomson was accomplished in the outdoors and had spent the previous five summers camping and painting on and around the Algonquin Park lake that, some people have concluded, claimed his life. A study of the events leading up to Thomson's death makes a conclusion of "death by accidental drowning" at best difficult to accept. Tom Thomson was more than likely murdered, either during or after a drinking party at a friend's cottage. Today, only his limited collection of paintings and his apparition remain.

People who have witnessed the vision of a man in a checked shirt paddling a distinctive grey-green canoe through the early morning mists by the shores of Canoe Lake are convinced that the spirit of Tom Thomson is still with us. Over the years, there have been many reports of such sightings. Considering that there is mystery surrounding both Thomson's death and his final resting place, it is not much wonder that his apparition merely vaporizes if anyone comes too close.

Thomson's remains were initially buried in a grave beside Canoe Lake. Not long afterward, his family asked that the casket be disinterred and shipped to the family plot many miles away. Whether or not this removal was actually accomplished has been a subject of debate ever since.

In 1956, four men, united by a fascination with the convoluted Tom Thomson legend, decided to disinter the man's original grave. They did discover a skeleton in a rotting casket, but it was that of a Native man, and therefore clearly not Thomson's. The implication is that in July 1917, the man's friends did properly comply with the family's wishes by shipping the coffin, body and all, to the family cemetery. Contradicting this premise, however, is that Thomson's original gravesite was tended by the woman he loved until the day she died. She obviously believed it to be Thomson's final resting place. Any children who accidentally ventured near the plot could be guaranteed a severe reprimand if they were spotted by the woman.

Given these circumstances, it isn't much wonder that Tom Thomson's ghost continues to paddle the lake he so loved in life. As with almost any ghost story, this one has attracted its fair share of skeptics. Nevertheless, over the years a great many reputable citizens have come forward to describe the apparition of Tom Thomson. Some, such as author Audrey Saunders and Judge William Little, have described the sightings in books that they have written.

All the ghostly reports are similar. Inevitably the witnesses are enjoying the tranquillity of Algonquin Park when a man, alone in a canoe, paddles into sight. Some of the witnesses have spoken to him and others have received a wave from him, but most people have just watched the man in the checked shirt beach his grey-green canoe—and then disappear into the mists of time.

The Northway family once hosted Group of Seven painter Lawren Harris, the last of the original Group of Seven artists to die, at their cottage on Smoke Lake. Mrs. Northway took the opportunity to recount for Harris her own encounter with the long-deceased Tom Thomson, who had been friends with most of the artists who went on to form the Group of Seven after his death. Mrs. Northway explained how she and a guide had spent a relaxing day fishing on the lake. By evening they were heading home. When the guide thought he saw someone nearby, he assumed that Mrs. Northway's family had come to meet them.

With a second look the man knew that he'd been mistaken, for the image of the man wearing the yellow checked shirt in a grey-green canoe vanished as quickly as it had appeared. Lawren Harris remained convinced for the rest of his life that what Mrs. Northway had seen and what many others had seen was, in fact, the spirit of his friend, Tom Thomson.

Both since and before Mrs. Northway's sighting, many people from all walks of life have been fascinated by the sight of a lone canoeist, clearly meeting the description of Tom Thomson, paddling silently through the rushes near the shore of Canoe Lake and then disappearing before their eyes.

Tom Thomson's ghost has been seen so often over the years that the legend has become as much an Ontario standard as are the man's distinctive landscape paintings.

Is It—or Isn't It— Haunted?

Great controversy swirls around the ghosts supposedly residing in Toronto's historically significant Mackenzie House. There are staunch proponents on each side of the debate.

The tales first became public in 1960 when the now-defunct Toronto *Telegram* ran a series of local ghost stories. In it, reporter Andrew MacFarlane published statements from the Edmunds, former caretakers at Mackenzie House. These reports were convincing, if only because none of the participants had anything to gain by fabricating the chronicles.

No reporter would risk his reputation by inventing a story of such questionable news value, and the Edmunds couldn't have expected their standing in the community to be enhanced by the publicity. Further, the descriptions that all members of the Edmunds family gave of their experiences with the spirits in Mackenzie House were detailed and not in the least contradictory of one another.

Mrs. Edmunds, who nowhere in any of the statements was accorded the dignity of a given name, apparently experienced one of the extremely rare episodes of phantom violence. She reported that in 1958, as she slept, an image that she had seen before appeared at the head of her bed. It hovered over her and then slapped her on the cheek, leaving her bruised.

This apparition may have been the same one that frightened the Edmunds' grandchildren when they stayed the night at the historic place. The children, who had been sleeping on the third

Mackenzie House is, according to many, home to spirits.

floor of Mackenzie House, made their way in the middle of the night to the second-floor bathroom. Seconds later their terrified shrieks brought every adult in the house running. They had seen the image of a woman in the small room, an image that vanished in a flash.

Mr. and Mrs. Edmunds each attested to the other's lack of interest in or knowledge of the history of the Mackenzie family, yet both described seeing "a little bald man in a frock coat." Although William Lyon Mackenzie, Toronto's first mayor and leader of the Rebellion of 1837, was bald throughout most of his adult life, he always wore a hairpiece in public. There are, therefore, no pictures showing him to be bald: this small but important fact supports the Edmunds' credibility.

The couple told of hearing footsteps on the stairs when there was no one near them; the sounds of music coming from an unoccupied room. These particular claims would be difficult to verify one way or the other. Phantom footsteps are a component of many, many ghost stories, and that the piano now in the restored house did not belong to the Mackenzies really doesn't prove anything at all. It is known that they were a musical family and that they owned a piano. The strains heard in the 1950s and 1960s could well have been residual energy, just as the sounds on the staircase might have been.

Two auditory manifestations that the Edmunds, and by extension the newspaper, probably misinterpreted were what they reported as the sounds of a toilet flushing and a printing press running. There wasn't a flush toilet in Mackenzie House when that family lived there, and the press that William Lyon Mackenzie used is known to make a distinctive noise and was most definitely not the one specified by the Edmunds.

Mackenzie House officials vehemently denied that there was any truth to the ghost stories about the house yet, oddly, proceeded to have the old place blessed by a member of the

Anglican clergy. The service must not have been entirely successful, as there were still reports of phantom sounds and images throughout the balance of the 1960s.

One of those images might have been tied to a specific piece of Canadian political history. After the failed Rebellion of 1837, John Montgomery, one of William Lyon Mackenzie's supporters, was sentenced to death by hanging. Upon hearing the court's decision, Montgomery cursed the men he said had given perjured testimony against him. He willed unnatural and early deaths to them all. The judgement against Montgomery was eventually commuted and he lived to be nearly one hundred. Two of those who testified against him later killed themselves.

Rounding out the stories of the Mackenzie family ghosts is William Lyon Mackenzie's grandson and namesake, William Lyon Mackenzie King, also a Canadian political leader— Canada's longest serving prime minister. He was a man who believed so strongly in the existence of spirits and his ability to contact them that he frequently held seances at Laurier House, his Ottawa home (see "Prime Minister Brought Spirit to Ottawa," p. 152).

The ghosts of the William Lyon Mackenzie legacy do not rest in peace.

Late for the Party

Peter Smith, with London's Eldon House, kindly took time one summer morning to relate the following classic Ontario ghost story. He began by explaining "We haven't seen him for over one hundred years but we do have the story anyway." This spine-chiller dates back to the earliest days of the elegant old residence.

"It was about 1842," Peter began. "Sarah, John Harris's eldest daughter, had a summer afternoon party to which a number of people were invited, including a young officer by the name of Wenman Weniatt. He was one of the invited guests [but] he didn't show up when he was expected to show up. However, at six o'clock in the evening, with the clock chiming in the hall, he was seen standing at the front door. He was spoken to by John Harris and he [Weniatt] didn't reply. He was spoken to by one of Sarah's sisters and he didn't reply. He was then seen by a number of guests to walk across the front of the house and down the west side until he was out of sight. The next day his servant arrived at the house and asked if they had seen the young officer. It was explained that he had been there but had acted rather strangely. They [had begun] discussing what to do when a local farmer came into town with a horse that he had found as a stray and [that] he recognized...as a garrison horse. They [the Harris family and Weniatt's servant] recognized it as Weniatt's horse [and] they sent out a search party. Later that afternoon they found his body on the banks of the Thames River near where the university stands today. He had been thrown from his horse, he had been killed and his watch had been smashed at six o'clock."

Chapter

GHOSTS OF THE GREAT LAKES

The *Edmund Fitzgerald*

A phantom ship, sometimes called a *Flying Dutchman* in reference to one of the oldest ghost ships, is an apparition of a sailing craft that has met a tragic end. The most frequently told version of the original *Flying Dutchman* legend involves a foolishly stubborn sea captain who insisted on continuing to sail around the Cape of Good Hope during a severe storm. The ship, her captain and her crew were all lost as a result of the man's perilous decision, and so his soul has been doomed to sail the ill-fated vessel into eternity. Sightings of her image have been reported over the years. Phantom ships are often seen during storms and are almost always associated with tragedy.

Occasionally, entire fleets of ghost ships have been reported. These armada appear only briefly and often seem to be floating just slightly above the waves. Scientists like to explain away this phenomenon by crediting a mirage effect caused by alternating layers of warm and cold air above the water. This layering, apparently, will cause an optical illusion—the appearance that a ship or group of ships is riding above the level of the water. Unfortunately, because many of the images reported are clearly from eras that are long past, the mirage theory does nothing to explain the sighting itself.

Perhaps the strangest of such sightings was witnessed by a group of sailors. It appeared to them to be a steamship encased in an enormous glass case moving along at a good pace, some distance above the water level.

According to the lyrics in one of Gordon Lightfoot's songs, the watery depths of Lake Superior can be tragically possessive. Of course, the musician didn't create that theory; Native tribes had been respectful of the lake's lethal grasp for generations. Lightfoot merely sang about the apparent hex in his tribute to the men lost when the *Edmund Fitzgerald* sank on November 10, 1975. Throughout the history and geography of shipping on the enormous and unpredictable body of water that is Lake Superior, there have been accounts of vessels vanishing without a trace.

Many of those vanished ships—including the *Edmund Fitzgerald*—have been sighted hours, weeks, years and even centuries after their demise—sighted as a phantom ship, that is.

The *Edmund Fitzgerald* certainly fits into those expected categories. Her sudden sinking has been studied by experts in the field of naval investigation. As she was within visual range of other ships, it is known that the *Edmund Fitzgerald*, an enormous ore carrier, sank completely beneath the surface of the water, and therefore from view, in less than two minutes. That short a time span would seem to defy accepted laws of physics and yet that is exactly what happened.

It is now reasoned that, although the *Edmund Fitzgerald*'s captain knew his ship had been damaged in the Lake Superior storm, he did not appreciate the extent or seriousness of that damage. If he had, surely he would have radioed for assistance. The facts that remain tell us that he did not and, mere seconds after a sailor on the nearby *Anderson* noted his position relative to the *Fitzgerald*'s, the largest ship ever to ply the Great Lakes simply disappeared from sight. All hands were lost.

For years, no physical trace of the ship was seen again. Her soul, however, continues to buffet her way through the waves— as a phantom ship, one of the most modern additions to the legions of ghost ships in Ontario.

The Ghost of the *Griffon*

One of the most enduring sightings of a phantom ship originated in the summer of 1679. The *Griffon*, under the command of the Cavalier de La Salle, was the first ship to sail on the Great Lakes and she was lost on its maiden voyage. Like the *Fitzgerald* centuries later, the *Griffon* was considered a giant. Both ships apparently vanished from the lake only to reappear as phantoms, occasionally seen by sailors, especially on foggy nights. The actual location of the *Fitzgerald* has, by now, been determined, whereas those who thought they knew where the *Griffon* lay have since been proven wrong.

The *Bannockburn*

Images of the *Bannockburn* were first reported within hours of her sinking in November 1902. The *Bannockburn* was a sturdy nine-year-old British-built steamer being used to carry grain to a port in Georgian Bay. If the ship's captain or crew had ever had any problems with the *Bannockburn*, they had not recorded them. It is presumed that the ship served the purpose for which she was designed and served it well—right up until the instant she went down, taking all hands with her and leaving virtually no trace that she had ever existed.

Just a few days after the *Bannockburn*'s disappearance, a Kingston newspaper reported, "It is generally conceded that the missing steamer is not within earthly hailing distance, that she has found an everlasting berth in the unexplored depths of Lake Superior, and that the facts of her foundering will never be known."

A considerably less romantically worded but more detailed report came from Captain James McMaugh, who was sailing aboard the *Algonquin*. McMaugh recalled that he saw the *Bannockburn* on the afternoon of November 21, 1902, "plugging along through choppy seas...." Immediately after noting the other ship's position in relation to his own, McMaugh looked briefly in another direction. Approximately three minutes later, he looked toward the *Bannockburn*'s location again and was surprised to note that the ship had vanished from sight. When interviewed several days later, McMaugh surmised that the other ship's boilers might have blown up in the few minutes that he'd looked away. Given the distance between the two ships and that the *Algonquin*'s hatches would all have been closed against the storm, McMaugh reasoned that he would not have heard the explosion. As no one could come up with a more plausible explanation, the experienced seaman's opinion was generally accepted as correct.

Even so, a confusing array of reports was received—some stemming from incidents just hours after the *Bannockburn* disappeared from Captain McMaugh's line of vision. Members of the crew serving on night watch aboard the *Huronic* stated that they'd seen the *Bannockburn* through the night of November 22. It wasn't until the *Huronic* made port six days later that the crew learned that the ship they had been so sure they'd seen had actually been at the bottom of the lake for several hours by the time they saw her image.

The reports from the *Huronic* were not unique. A Fort William newspaper quoted a grain elevator superintendent named Sellars as saying he'd seen the *Bannockburn* near Slate Island. The man withdrew his statement shortly after, perhaps not wanting to be thought of as someone prone to "seeing things." He need not have worried. A mere sighting of the phantom *Bannockburn* would soon seem mundane compared to other, extremely detailed, reports being filed.

One of the most convoluted and involved sightings came from the crew of the ship *Germanic*. Sailors aboard that ship reported to the Marine Insurance Company of Chicago that the *Bannockburn* had not, in fact, sunk because they had seen her ashore. After one such sighting of the *Bannockburn*'s manifestation, even the federal government was advised that the ship was fine and only stranded in an isolated location. The crews' families were also given this information, pointlessly buoying their hopes.

As the sightings of the phantom ship collected and the days passed without direct contact, concern grew. Search parties were sent out to the spots where the *Bannockburn* had been reported. One tug came back with a report of a great deal of debris in an area where there had been a sighting, but that was all.

Scuttlebutt among Great Lakes' deckhands became ominous. The superstitious sailors knew then that what was being reported was a ship that would never make port again, a ghost ship doomed to ply Lake Superior's waters into eternity.

Months later a single oar and a life preserver were picked up and identified as belonging to the *Bannockburn*. Nothing more was ever found, but the phantom sightings that began just hours after she sank have continued over the years. As Dwight Boyer put it in his book, *Ghost Ships of the Great Lakes*, "On stormy nights several sailors claimed to have seen the *Bannockburn* buffeting her way down Lake Superior, her lamps blinking in the storm scud while in the darkened pilothouse her master looked vainly for the welcoming [shore]."

A Phantom near Toronto Harbour

In August 1910, a well-documented ghost ship sighting occurred and was painstakingly recorded by Great Lakes historian Rowley W. Murphy. What makes this particular event especially dramatic is that the phantom ship was not only seen but also heard.

It seems that a group of eleven men, Murphy included, had set out for a sail upon Lake Ontario on a summer's night. At nightfall they sheltered just west of Toronto Harbour. All hands were sound asleep for the night when they were aroused by a repetitive whistling, which they recognized as coming from another lake-going vessel.

Once up on deck, Murphy and his mates could clearly see an old-fashioned clipper ship complete with oil lamps burning in some of the windows. As experienced sailors themselves, the awakened men knew the repetitive signals meant the ship they saw was in distress. Puzzled, but ready to respond, the docked party sent out a contingent of men in a small dinghy to offer what assistance they could.

Moments later, the party of supposed rescuers arrived at the spot where the image had been seen. There was nothing there. The moon was full and bright, making for good visibility, and so there could be no doubt—the lake was empty—there was no ship, in distress or otherwise.

Chapter

GHOSTS
IN PUBLIC

Enduring Eternity

In the summer of 1873, the town of Whitby was abuzz with talk of a ghost. The story even hit the newspapers and spread throughout most of Ontario. "A GHOST IN WHITBY" the article's headline proclaimed. Under that, a subhead added, "THE APPARITION SEEN AND DESCRIBED."

"The [newspaper] editor was a little bit cheeky about it," chuckled Whitby archivist Brian Winter. "He thought it was all a bunch of nonsense. You can tell by the way he wrote it up."

Despite the local media's tongue-in-cheek approach (the article once referred to the presence as "his ghostship"), Winter added, "People stayed up all night sitting in the courtroom waiting for [the entity] to come out."

What makes this ghost story even more intriguing are the manifestation's different appearances. "The apparition...is seen under various forms [including] that of a black dog, which suddenly assumes the shape of a rather tall man... [with] eyes [that are] burning red flames. Others said they saw the ghost leaning on a staff, standing on the courthouse steps moaning sorrowfully and [they] claimed it turned to flame and disappeared into the ground when they approached," according to the newspaper account. To complete the theatrics, this ghost knew exactly when to make an entrance: at "the witching hour."

Eventually all the excitement over the presence quieted down and life in and around Whitby returned to normal. By 1964, after the old, once-haunted building had served as the area's courthouse for 110 years, the justice system moved out of it. In 1967 the city chose the building as a Centennial project and

The former Ontario County Courthouse is now the Whitby Centennial Building, and it is still haunted.

renovated it into a community centre that included a theatre. About that time the ghostly activity began again.

One report indicated that the lights in the building would turn on and off when no one was near them. Others indicated a much stronger presence than that.

"In the 1970s there was a theatre group in the old courtroom and some of them actually saw a figure of a person floating down from the balcony," Brian Winter recalled, before adding that the caretaker frequently had his dog with him in the building. "The animal would sniff around the door to the balcony and wag its tail as if there was something there. I think it was 1988 [when] the local newspaper did an article. They brought in some psychics and [the psychics] came up with a story...that a man fell over the balcony and fell to his death. I've never found any documented proof of that happening. You'd think that would have been reported in the papers but the problem is we're missing a lot of papers because of fires [that burned all known copies of those issues]. The [ghost] was in an old-fashioned costume so it must have happened many, many years ago."

The psychics related that this haunting dated back to a trial in the 1800s and that the ghost was the uncle of a man who was once on trial for rape.

"They [the psychics] told him [the uncle] he was dead and could go on his way," Winter remembered. "I don't know if anybody has seen it [the ghost] since then."

Hopefully, the exorcism was successful and the soul that haunted the old courthouse building in Whitby has, by now, found his eternal rest.

Spirits with Your Meal?

A long time ago in Toronto, one particular family was so revered that a popular saying developed around their name. It went something like this—"In Toronto there are no classes, only the Masseys and the masses." The rigid class structure that existed at that time in Ontario's capital city has deteriorated considerably by now, but there is still no denying the importance the members of the Massey family played in Canadian history. Daniel Massey began a company from which his son Hart built the enormous Massey-Ferguson Limited. Vincent Massey became the country's first native-born governor general, and his brother Raymond became a renowned actor. All used their wealth and power to support what was then a developing arts scene in Canada. Many of the institutions that Torontonians take for granted today would not exist were it not for the farsightedness and generosity of Masseys.

Their legacy apparently also lives on in another dimension.

Michael Ratz, former general manager of the Keg Mansion at 515 Jarvis Street in downtown Toronto, is perhaps more aware than most people of the extent to which that particular aspect of the Massey legacy exists. While Ratz still worked at the Keg Mansion, I asked him about any possible encounters with the ghosts rumoured to haunt the beautiful old building that was once home to the Massey family and he replied without any hesitation.

"I've had some personal experience, yes. I spend a lot of time in this building. I've been the only person here in the middle of the night with the lights off...and I'm very comfortable with it. The ghosts are friendly," he explained calmly.

"Ghosts?" I inquired. "You used the plural. Is there more than one ghost?"

"Well, yes," the personable host continued. "There's a number of them. I don't think it's one ghost. I guess the most popular ghost is one of the maids. Mrs. [Lillian] Massey, who was confined to a wheelchair in her later days, went through a lot of ill-health. The help lived in the house...so they were quite close [to the family members] and when Mrs. Massey died there was one of the maids who was so overcome with grief that she hanged herself from the oval vestibule over the main foyer.

I haven't seen that one [but] the story goes that from time to time a hanging spectre can be seen."

Not all the spirits around the Victorian mansion are quite that dramatic. Ratz classes the other presences as "interesting" and allows that someone with a different perspective would, perhaps, credit coincidence rather than entities from beyond.

"There are interesting little things, not necessarily at night. Nothing substantive; some may say it could happen anywhere, some may say, oh no, that's been influenced by another power," he elaborated.

There have been sightings of a small boy bounding up the staircase and laughter has been heard coming from the upper floors where the children's quarters were located during the Massey era. Pat Murphy, who was employed by the Keg during the 1980s, explained that in the early spring of 1988, while working alone in the building, he distinctly heard a little boy's voice calling "Mommy, mommy, I'm over here." That was probably the voice of the same apparition that ran past a bartender when the man was sure he was alone in the building.

In keeping with many ghost stories, one or more of the spirits residing in the mansion enjoys tinkering with both the lights and the sound system—both come on and go off by themselves.

Horace King, who worked as an overnight cleaner at the restaurant, claims to have seen the ghost of Mrs. Massey on more than one occasion.

The incident that Ratz found most intriguing, however, did not concern the Massey family at all. Prior to 1976, when the restaurant became the flagship of the Keg chain, the former Massey home was a different restaurant and "a pretty hip place," as Ratz put it.

"It was called Julie's Mansion and Jules Fine was the operator...in the '60s. The bar upstairs was called the Bombay Bicycle Club and he was the guy who was running it."

The Keg—good food and great ghosts are on the menu in this restaurant.

The flamboyant Mr. Fine not only loved the ladies but loved to draw attention to himself. In contrast, he specifically created the restaurant as a place where the rich and the famous could enjoy an evening out, knowing that they were not going to be the target of unwanted attention. Fine was once quoted as saying, "Our whole idea here is to leave celebrated people alone. [Former governor general] Vincent Massey is the only person who ever made a big stir. When he walked into the dining room, everybody got up and applauded."

The restaurant concept was tremendously successful and the business ran until Fine closed the place in the fall of 1975. Within one year, the Keg opened at the same address. Several years after that, Michael Ratz took over as the restaurant's general manager.

On a cold day early in 1997, twenty-two years after giving up the 515 Jarvis Street address, Jules Fine died. On that very day, Mike Ratz wonders if Mr. Fine might have made one final entrance to the building that he once owned and ran so successfully. For, after all those years, on the very day of the older man's death, Ratz received a letter addressed to the colourful Toronto icon.

If you're interested in a great meal surrounded by Canadian history, the Keg Mansion is the place to go—that much is a guarantee. With luck, it'll be served with an image of the past as a side dish.

Riding into Eternity

Producers of grade B slasher-horror movies must never have heard the Legend of Ghost Road or they would have arrived on Scugog Island in droves. This truly spooky story really has it all—danger, death and a very eerie apparition. For lovers of true ghost stories, the Scugog Township tale has an even more impressive component—readily visible phantom lights that follow a predictable sequence.

It's difficult to pin down when the sightings began. Some say it was as recently as the early 1980s, others think they remember hearing about the phantom motorcycle rider as far back as the 1960s. The origin of the paranormal phenomenon is a tragic tale. A young man was riding his motorcycle at excessive speed. He lost control of the bike and was thrown to his death. Now, it seems, he's doomed to make that drive forever.

The motorcycle's headlight is always seen heading in one direction. As it passes you, it disappears and is almost immediately replaced by the image of a smaller red tail-light. Locals reason that the ghost is driving over and over the strip of road that claimed his life.

Not only are the images amazingly consistent, but so are the reports from psychics witnessing the event. Unknown to one another, they have described the motorcycle rider as a man in his early twenties, with sandy brown hair, wearing a gold-coloured motorcycle helmet. One even went so far as to suggest the ghost's name was either Dan or Dave Sweeney.

The predictability of the manifestation's appearances has drawn crowds of both believers and skeptics. Those looking for a matter-of-fact interpretation almost always base their explanation on headlights reflecting from decidedly physical sources—that is, simply other traffic. That rationalization even holds up—some of the time. It falls apart completely, though, when the weather closes in and visibility becomes so poor that you can't see an approaching or retreating vehicle's lights. But you can still see the phantom motorcyclist.

Capturing the image of a ghost on film or video is never easy, but a team of students from the film studies program at a nearby college succeeded in doing exactly that—not just once but twice. The first shot was taken by a still camera. When the exposure was developed, the basketball-sized light that the student had observed firsthand appeared to actually be a human form aglow in a strong, white aura. If that were not amazing enough, a video taken at the site revealed the same image but much more clearly. Details of the ghostly body can, reportedly, actually be made out.

Animals are considerably more sensitive to the presence of spirits than are human beings. For this reason, area skeptics are usually a little puzzled when the pet dog who had been riding contentedly beside them on the seat of the car suddenly becomes anxious at the approach to the haunted strip of highway.

A skeptical journalist learned a new lesson in reality when he and others made their way out to Ghost Road. Hoping to disprove the legend once and for all, the group split up—half of the people staying at the most northerly stretch of the affected roadway and the other half of the group making their way to the far end of the predictable route. They were equipped with both walkie-talkies and CB radios.

No sooner had the far group assembled than they saw a glow of white off where their counterparts were. Thinking the others were using their car headlights as a visual signal establishing an exact location on the deserted road, the people at the other end radioed that they had a fix on the headlights and that their colleagues could turn them off now so as not to drain the battery. The response was enough to chill even the most confirmed skeptic. "We don't have our lights on."

Is it any wonder that people drive from the surrounding countryside and some even come up from the States to witness the Scugog Island ghost rider?

Haunted Jails

It's difficult to understand why anyone would want to stay in a jail longer than they absolutely had to but, strangely, the places are notoriously frequently haunted. Alcatraz, the island

Once called a "Palace for Prisoners," the Don Jail now serves as a home to ghosts.

penitentiary in the San Francisco Bay, is rumoured to be home to spirits of deceased convicts even though it has not been used as a jail for many years.

In Ontario, at least two jails are also haunted. David St. Onge, curator of the Correctional Service Museum of Canada, supplied the following brief but grim history of the Kingston Penitentiary since its opening on June 1, 1835.

"No less than five officers have been murdered by inmates here....In all honesty, we have yet to tabulate the number of inmates who have died 'within the walls.' During the nineteenth century, epidemics such as cholera and typhoid were not uncommon and, as you can imagine, were devastating in such confined quarters."

Having set the stage, the curator went on to explain that "many of our present staff have made reference to 'feelings' that they get in certain areas of the institution." He added, however, that the majority of those people experiencing such feelings are either hesitant or unable to "give...any more detail."

"The museum itself is located across the street from the prison proper, in the old Warden's Residence, which was first occupied in 1873. I have confirmed that the first warden that resided here, John Creighton, passed away here in 1885 after an illness. His funeral was held in the parlour (now one of the display rooms) and he was then taken directly to the cemetery for interment. I believe that his passing was not such that his spirit would be 'condemned to walk the earth,' however…there have been some occurrences at the museum that beg explanation," St. Onge acknowledged.

"Often I find myself working into the night. On various occasions I have heard doors slam, floorboards creaking and the like but have always been able to rationalize the cause (cross-breezes off Lake Ontario through open windows, etc.)," the man revealed.

It was clear, though, that his rationalization process has, after some events, broken down completely.

"I have also thought that I have heard voices calling my name or saying 'hello' on more than one occasion. Usually, it has been a faint voice, but it has been enough to cause me to get up from my desk to see if anyone is downstairs at the entrance of the museum."

St. Onge also indicated that there have been records kept of at least one ghost sighting in the prison. Apparently, in the nineteenth century, an inmate claimed the ghost of his mother had visited him in his cell (which the curator points out was only seventy-four centimetres wide and 2.4 metres long) and concluded that anecdote with the comment, "It appears that this claim was largely disregarded by the authorities at the time and was attributed to insanity. The inmate was transferred to an asylum in Lower Canada."

If the accommodations at the asylum were more spacious than at the jail, the inmate might have been more wily than insane.

The ghost at the "palace for prisoners," as Toronto's Don Jail was once called, is that of a woman prisoner. The haunted section of the jail is no longer in use so it's difficult to tell if the apparition of the blonde woman still roams the halls. She was a suicide victim whose spirit was frequently seen in the rotunda area of the old prison.

Perhaps the detractor who made the comparison between the Don Jail and a palace had noted that the cells in the newer Toronto institution were a generous thirteen centimetres wider than those in the older Kingston Pen. Apparently, though, the extra space was no guarantee that the jail would stand ghost-free for all time.

The International Hostel in downtown Ottawa is a most unusual facility in that it used to be the Nicholas Street Jail. Amazingly, there have been very few structural changes made to accommodate its conversion. The bars and forbidding stone walls are still in place: the prisoners' cells have simply become travellers' bedrooms.

At one time the hostel offered a free night's accommodation to anyone who was able to spend the entire night in the cell that was once assigned to house death-row prisoners during their last night before death. To date, no one's been able to collect on that offer because, not surprisingly, the tiny, inhospitable-looking room is very haunted.

The most common apparition is thought to be that of Patrick James Whelan, the man convicted of assassinating D'Arcy McGee. Whelan professed his innocence all the way to the gallows in 1869 and, today, many people assume he was guilty only of being drunk and in the wrong place at the wrong time. Although his anger would be justified, Whelan doesn't seem to be vengeful. He merely repeats his last actions on earth over and over again.

Those folks brave enough to try staying in the death-row cell were very consistent in their reports of the supernatural occurrences that they witnessed. They said that they were awakened by the sensation that someone has just sat down on their bed. Some saw a figure sitting on the bed with his head in his hands. Others simply sensed a presence. After the ghost had sat for a moment, it stood and moved toward the cell door. Once that entity was in the hallway, another presence joined the first and they'd move down the corridor toward the gallows area.

Although not everyone actually saw the ghost, most visitors reported that they had heard disembodied voices reciting the Lord's Prayer. (Researcher Alice d'Anjou confirms that her studies show that when Whelan was taken from his cell by a priest, they repeated that prayer as they made their way down the hall.) These voices were usually enough to drive even the most skeptical running for some human company. Unfortunately, that particular bit of comfort was not always available because it is at this point in the ghostly ordeal that people often discovered that they were "locked" into the cell. Although the locks had been removed many years ago, so that it was physically impossible for the doors to lock, that information probably didn't buy the distraught guest much consolation. The situation was taken seriously enough that, out of concern for the possibility of someone becoming trapped in there, the fire department has now forbidden the hostel from renting out the death-row cell.

But Whelan is not the only phantom in the old jail. A less frequent visitor from beyond creates a sudden icy and isolated gust of air around the guests. Some hostel guests have also felt a cold, clammy hand touch them, and many report the distinct sensation of evil being directed at them.

Upstairs, the area that used to house the women prisoners, their children and children who'd been incarcerated, is now a television lounge. Guests report hearing phantom sounds of mournful "crying children" and "noisy families" even though there are rarely such people billeted in the hostel.

There are probably more spirits in the old building, but they are somewhat nondescript and therefore difficult to identify—doors will slam closed and windows will open on their own. One particularly eerie window is four floors up. Because it had no bars on it, there were escape attempts through that window—most ended in death on the hard ground below.

The International Hostel in downtown Ottawa has, tragically, earned its ghostly legacy.

Haunted or Not?

According to a 1988 article in the *Toronto Star*, the Royal Ontario Museum (ROM) was included in a ghost tour organized by a former archaeologist named Bette Shepherd. The story indicated that the museum building was home to at least two ghosts—the apparition of a little blonde girl dressed in white and an old man dressed as though ready to retire for the night. The latter image was apparently presumed to be the ghost of Dr. Charles Currelly, a former long-time director of the museum.

In order to follow up on the lead provided by the newspaper article, I wrote a letter to the museum inquiring as to whether there'd been any recent ghost sightings. Ellen Flowers of the museum's media relations department answered my query.

Oddly, she wrote, "No one here at the ROM has ever heard of either a ghost of Dr. Currelly or a little girl."

The contradictory reports are certainly provocative.

A Ghost Makes the Newspaper

It was a beautiful September evening, the last Sunday of the month. The residents of St. Catharines were out enjoying "Indian summer" at its very finest. The temperature was comfortably warm, the sun had not yet set and just a hint of a breeze stirred the trees.

Three men, good friends all, stood in front of Voisard's grocery store passing the time away chatting aimlessly. Just as one man made a comment, a movement in the periphery of another man's vision drew his attention from the conversation at hand to the buildings lining the street on which the little group stood.

He gasped in surprise and horror as he spotted the movement that had distracted him. He could hardly believe his eyes. There was a man walking on the edge of the roof of a nearby building.

"That man will fall and be killed," the man cried as he pointed to the figure high above.

By now, all three men were staring intently at the figure. There could be no question about what they were seeing, for the man's image was clearly outlined against the cloudless sky. What was odder still was that the man appeared to be nearly 2.4 metres tall and was holding a long pole above his head, apparently to help him maintain his precarious balance.

The three men watched, paralysed in horrified fascination, as the image turned from the edge of the roof and made his way up to the peak. The witnesses began to run to the building to offer assistance but stopped when they realized that the apparition had now shrunk considerably in size. Again they stood stock still for a moment. Then, all of a sudden, the spectre vanished completely.

Thinking that the man had fallen and would most certainly require first aid, the three would-be rescuers rushed first to the sides and finally to the back of the building. Oddly, there was no one there at all, much less an injured roof-walker with a pole. The image had not fallen, but had simply vanished.

The men were aghast. They did not know either what to think or what to do. Deciding that not much would be gained from reporting the incident to the police, the three went to the local newspaper office, where they relayed information about their sighting. Their descriptions of the event were amazingly similar, right down to the clothing worn by the presence that they'd seen on the roof. None could account for the sudden and strange appearance of the man with the pole any more easily than for his equally sudden and strange disappearance.

Their report was first written up in the St. Catharines Star and then copied by the Toronto World. Under the double headline of "WAS IT A GHOST?" and "ST. CATHARINES EXCITED OVER A ROPE-WALKING SPOOK," a nameless reporter confirmed that "A sharp watch has been kept on the spot [where the phantom was sighted] since, but the spectacle has not reappeared. The neighborhood is greatly excited over the incident and many speculations are indulged in as to a solution of the mystery."

Unfortunately, the nameless scribe either did not know, or simply chose not to reveal, the nature of those speculations. In case you're tempted to scoff about the quality of today's newspaper reporting, you should probably note that the article's dateline was October 3, 1890.

A Ghostly Heritage

Architecturally speaking, Cherry Hill House Restaurant in Mississauga certainly doesn't blend into the neighbourhood. This incongruity, however, only adds dignity to both the stately old building and the attractive modern homes that surround it.

The history of Cherry Hill House dates back to the early 1800s, when it was built on crown land granted to Joseph and Jane Silverthorn. The couple lived there for the balance of their lives before leaving the place to their daughters. The last surviving Silverthorn daughter willed the house to an eccentric nephew who was too busy with his acting career to pay too much attention to the old home. He rented the place to a family named Lindsey (or possibly Lindsay), and many people believe it is Mr. Lindsey's spirit that still roams the charming place, seemingly unaware of either his own death or the home's successful conversion to a popular restaurant.

The only record of Lindsey's spirit having been seen is not a reliable one, for the sighting might only have been the result of a practical joke. The incident took place in the 1970s, shortly after the house had been moved to its current location. The move was the first step in the mammoth undertaking of converting the badly dilapidated Cherry Hill House into an attractive restaurant. Wanting to protect their investment, the new owners hired a night watchman. The poor man was badly frightened one night when he thought caught a glimpse of a ghostly intruder.

Nearly twenty years later, the perpetrator of the hoax came forward to confess. He had been part of the crew that had moved the old place. After an evening that included a few beers with his workmates, the man decided it would be fun to scare the security guard into thinking the house was haunted. He explained that he would have come forward and confessed to the prank earlier except that he'd noticed that local newspapers had reported the story as a news event, and he was concerned, with great justification, that he might be charged with mischief.

There are people who feel that event alone is responsible for the legend of Cherry Hill House Restaurant's ghost. Others, however, don't think that one practical joke in 1973 is an adequate explanation for all the ghostly activity reported to have occurred throughout the converted building.

When the conversion work was being done, electricians were frequently disturbed to find that work they'd completed one day had been disassembled by the time they got back to the job site the next day. They were extremely puzzled, especially considering that the place was patrolled by security guards twenty-four hours per day. As many of the workers had heard ghostly sounds such as whistling and whispering throughout the house, they wondered if an unseen force might be playing the destructive pranks.

The security guards were not always the only ones at the house overnight. At least once, a worker who'd toiled well into the night had to be back at work early the next day. He decided that, rather than spending time driving to and from the job site and home, he would simply "camp out" in a corner of the restaurant. He was just falling asleep when he began to feel that he was no longer alone. When the man looked up he could see images "coming out of the fireplace and they appeared to be Indians."

The blocks that supported the newly moved building came from a field that had, according to an archaeological survey, been a Native burial ground, so this image was understandable but startling. Since then, these particular ghosts have been seen by others, and one worker is sure that one of them actually grabbed his shoulder.

One security guard gave a detailed report of the image of a young girl dressed in white riding past the house on a white horse. According to one of the psychics who was brought in later, there are many ghosts in the house. One is a girl named Miranda who burned to death in the house while making candles. The guard may have seen this girl.

Tom Skrela, the restaurant's manager, seems to be a man of pragmatic nature who tends to be skeptical about references to anything to do with ghosts and the like. The phantom footsteps that are occasionally heard from an empty upper storey do not impress him. Whatever drove two of his valued employees out into the night, however, did give Skrela pause to reflect.

It seems that one night Skrela was going through the closing-up procedures with the two women employees on staff that night. He finished his duties first, bid his employees a good night and headed home. As the workers left behind were among his best, Skrela had no qualms about leaving them responsible for the final lock-up.

Unfortunately, that night anyway, his confidence was not well placed. Not long after his departure, the women were terrified by the sounds of heavy footsteps emanating from the second storey of the restaurant—an area that they knew full well to be vacant. The two dropped what they'd been doing and fled from the house, convinced that the ghost was about to make his way down the stairs to where they were working.

Although the women's report was similar to others that the skeptical manager had heard, he took this one very seriously, for these particular employees were hard-working, sensible people who had been with him for a long time. He knew and trusted them. They were not the type to be given to irresponsible acts or flights of fancy. The women had definitely heard something legitimately perturbing.

The mysterious sounds that night have never been satisfactorily explained. Perhaps, on that particular night, the ghost of old man Lindsey merely thought it was late enough and therefore his turn to once again roam throughout his former residence.

Whatever the case may be, the events that night resulted in making it extremely difficult for at least three people to maintain any sort of an attitude of unthinking skepticism. The unexplainable late night noises from the empty second storey soon became accepted as a matter of course.

Skrela also told reporters about the jukebox that once complemented Cherry Hill's downstairs area. It seems that the machine would occasionally begin to play even when no one was around it.

All reports indicate that the Cherry Hill hauntings may be past their prime by now, as encounters are becoming more and more rare. Perhaps if you go there today, all you can expect at the Cherry Hill Restaurant is a delicious meal in elegant surroundings that were once home to ghosts.

George Still Roams

The building that now houses Kings Landing Steak and Seafood House on Park Street in Kingsville was constructed in 1863 as an inn named Elliott House. The location was chosen by David Elliott to take advantage of a newly constructed boat dock. The strategy paid off, and Elliott House soon became a popular spot for the sailors and lumberjacks using the nearby docking facilities.

David Elliott lived for nearly one hundred years but, by the time he died in 1918, his once-thriving establishment had become run down. After his death, it sat empty for many years, except for the clandestine residency of rumrunners during Prohibition. After that, the place was left to crumble until 1945, when new owners, the Pearces, opened a tavern in the former inn. Shortly after they took the place over, the Pearces realized that they'd bought more than just a piece of commercial real estate: they'd also acquired a ghost.

The Pearces' pets, a dog named Bruce and a cat whose name has not been recorded, would react to something that their owners could not see.

"Bruce would sometimes withdraw growling with his hair on end," according to the current owners of the haunted building. As for the cat, it would not stay in the place. If someone tried to bring it in, it would hiss violently and run back outside.

The humans were also made aware of the presence. They'd frequently hear footsteps echoing across the empty second floor. They were often puzzled to find lights that they knew had been turned off were now back on or, conversely, those that they'd turned on had mysteriously been turned off.

The resident spirit came to be known by the name "George." Although the ghost never did anyone any harm, he may have occasionally been hard on human pride, as he apparently did not like having the bathroom door shut. When he found it that way, he would open it. In addition, George clearly has no respect for thrift or conservation, as he will turn water taps on and let them run.

Possibly the most direct contacts George has made with the living are his reported cold, clammy touches, which a few people have claimed to have felt. As no one seems to know for sure exactly who George was when he was alive, these gestures might just be his way of introducing himself to the living. The current owners, staff and customers quite enjoy the extra presence at the eatery, but there are still a few people working there today who are not keen on being on the second floor of the restaurant by themselves.

And so, if you're looking for a little extra zing with your meal, be sure to visit Kings Landing Steak and Seafood House in Kingsville. George and the others will be delighted to have your company.

A Haunted Hospital

Considering its history, it would be disappointing if the War Memorial Hospital in Perth did not have at least one ghost story associated with it. The building began life in 1852, as Victoria Hall, the home of Judge John Glass Malloch.

During construction of the home, some of the building materials Malloch ordered were delivered late. The unscrupulous judge was said to have agreed to the delay at first, but then refused to pay for the supplies when they did arrive. However, the magistrate still incorporated them into his palatial home.

There was no point in the supplier taking legal action, for the man he would be suing would be the judge on his own case. No, the wronged man would have to take the situation to a much higher court. And he did. He laid a curse on the judge and his family; an apparently successful and fatal curse. He deemed that until the house built with ill-gotten materials was transformed into a building designated for the good of the community, the owners would suffer ill-health and premature death. From that day on, no one in the Malloch clan ever enjoyed good health and within forty years there were no descendants left alive. The home was left to the community to serve as a hospital— a purpose that effectively lifted the curse.

However, it is reported that the spirits of the Malloch family are still occasionally seen at second-storey windows and roaming the upstairs hallways. Fortunately, their disturbing images—even in death they appear cursed and sickly looking—don't bother anyone.

The Ghost is Gone

It seems that having a ghost in residence is not necessarily a permanent situation. A place that is haunted during one period of time might not always be haunted. The ghost may eventually leave or may only have been "passing through." Single ghostly visitations have also been documented. Therefore, just because a building is haunted today, doesn't mean that such will always be the case. Next year, next month or even tomorrow that same structure might well be a "ghost-free" zone. While such a theory may be reassuring to some people, it should be remembered that the opposite is also probably true: even if there are no spirits in your house today, there might be tomorrow.

The haunted status of Dundurn Castle in Hamilton now seems to fit into the category of "previously haunted." The stately old mansion was built by Sir Allan MacNab, a wealthy political, military and business leader during the mid-nineteenth century. For over one hundred years after MacNab's death in 1862, the castle served many functions for the community before being restored in 1967 as a Centennial project.

According to reports, there was ghostly activity noted during the Christmas season of 1988. Katherine Killins, who was the head historical interpreter at the time, recalled seeing the last Candlelight Tour visitor to the door. Killins walked through the house to make sure that the candles were all extinguished and that all was secure in the building. On this particular evening, when she reached the top floor, she could hear singing.

For just a second, perhaps distracted by other thoughts, the interpreter simply enjoyed the music. Then it struck her—she was alone in the building that she knew so well. But she realized that she was hearing music and that it was definitely coming from the inside of the house. Killins reported that she hadn't been frightened of the phantom songstress—just surprised.

Nearly ten years later, Bill Nesbitt, the current curator at Dundurn Castle, merely sounded nonplussed when asked about the existence of ghosts in his workplace.

"I don't know about a ghost," he laughed. "I've been here since '89. I've worked at other sites...at Mackenzie House and [ghost stories] are pretty routine there but nothing here like that. Nothing beyond the odd weird noise and creaking floorboards, but that's pretty standard [in an old building].

Perhaps the ghost Katherine Killins heard singing on that December evening in 1988 simply stayed on for a while after enjoying the Candlelight Tour with those of flesh and blood.

The Haunted Ghost Town

The Long Dog Reserve, near Big Trout Lake, is just about as far north as civilization gets in Ontario and, for a while in 1995, even this northern reserve was not occupied. The entire population (twenty residents in all) had, at their own request, been airlifted out of the tiny community.

Terror spread through the families at Long Dog shortly after the death of a woman who'd been "either a relative or close friend of everyone on the reserve" a Canadian Press story reported. The woman had died of natural causes, so it wasn't so much the death itself that had the others concerned, but their conviction that the woman's ghost was roaming around the settlement.

The frightened survivors reported seeing an apparition walking about holding a candle. Other reports included people hearing noises that sounded as though someone was inside a house when they knew for sure that that particular house was empty. Outsiders were quick to presume that the "ghost" was more accurately a grief reaction that had gained drama as it made its way through the tightly knit community. Of course, none of the people making that disclaimer had been at Long Dog Reserve when the dead woman's restless soul was stirring.

Mistress of the Mill

Watson's Mill in Manotick, near Ottawa, has been an area landmark for nearly 140 years. Amazingly, it's been haunted for nearly as long as it's existed. The mill was built and began operation in 1860. Entrepreneur Joseph Currier was proud of his partnership in the growing milling business and was anxious to show the state-of-the-art machinery to his bride Anna (or Ann, or Annie).

Tragically, Currier's pride and exuberance brought him nothing but heartache—a bit of the fabric from the billowing skirts that swirled about Anna's ankles got caught on a piece of working machinery, catapulting her against a supporting post and killing her instantly.

Joseph was devastated by the accident and his loss. It is interesting that while he gave up all interest in the building and the business from that point on, his wife has never left the place.

Reports of possible ghostly activity began not long after the tragedy occurred, and they continue right up to the present day.

One of the earliest recorded encounters dates back to the 1920s, when a fisherman sheltered from bad weather in the mill. He fled into the storm after hearing the ghostly cries of a woman's voice.

Often the ghostly encounters begin with the sounds of phantom moaning heard emanating from the mill. At other times, the first indication that something unnatural is about to occur is a loud *thump*. Sometimes those noises are the only way in which the long-deceased Anna's manifestation makes herself known. On occasion, her image can actually be seen at a second-storey window. Descriptions of the vision have been strikingly similar for more than a century—a white shadow of a woman wearing a long dress. She's been seen to move from one upstairs window to the next as if watching with interest the people who are observing her with equally great interest.

The *Manotick Messenger* recently asked clairvoyant Connie Adams to use her skills in detecting whether or not the old mill really is haunted. The results of her investigation were dramatic. Adams immediately sensed the woman's presence and was even able to pick out the whereabouts of the spirit in the building. As soon as Adams located the presence, she was able to "see" the woman as youthful and having dark-coloured hair. Anna indicated that she was happy and saw herself as being something of a guardian over the mill. The ghost even entertains occasionally, when a young girl's spirit visits her.

In common with many entities, Anna is distressed about some renovations that have been planned. Many ghosts become perturbed when the building that they haunt is altered in any way. For Anna, the concern is for a specific section of a basement wall. She informed the clairvoyant that there is something sealed in the wall that should be displayed as soon as it's been located.

Until the work begins, there is no way of knowing whether the spirit has a real concern. It's also possible that the psychic misinterpreted something or perhaps the ghost is setting her corporeal counterparts on a wild-goose chase.

Film producers Alice d'Anjou and Shannon Fisher decided to include the story of the mill in their documentary about hauntings in the Ottawa area. The ghost made her presence in the mill more than apparent during the production. Alice explained that, when they first arrived at the building, they weren't too familiar with the story and did not know which interior post had caused the young woman's death.

"When we were filming we just picked a likely looking post (mostly because it had good lighting and some room for the camera to move around). However, at one point I was 'blocking out' a scene (i.e., walking the path the actor would follow for the camera man) and got very suddenly chilled—goose bumps, and short of breath—the proverbial hair stood up on my neck. It caught me completely by surprise, I might add. I was not thinking about the ghost, [but] just how we were going to make a difficult shot work. I must have gasped out loud because 'Annie' [the spirit of the dead bride] asked me what was wrong. I said 'I don't know.' I took a step back and felt fine. When I stepped forward again it was like walking into a freezer. 'Annie' was very uncomfortable in that spot too and we did the shot as fast as we could and moved to another spot," Alice explained, before adding, "We later confirmed with the curator that that was indeed the deadly post."

It is not unusual for spirits to interfere with a story being filmed in "their" building, and Anna and the mill proved to be no exception.

"We had some strange lighting effects on the final film. [The camera operator] could not explain [them]," Alice said. "Everyone felt very odd during this shoot. Shannon's two children were with us that day. Emily, eighteen months at the time, was normally happy and active. She was fine on the drive down and home but anxious and clingy during the shoot. Jacob, nine years, usually enjoys that kind of outing too but was asking to leave within about fifteen minutes of arriving—'I just don't like it here,' he said."

A gentleman named Larry Ellis was visiting the mill to research a story he was going to write about the haunting. As he stood near a display that explains about Anna's spirit in the mill, he could feel but not see a presence standing directly behind him. While there he reported that he suddenly "broke out in goose bumps." He noted that this experience occurred at 1:15 p.m. Another man, cleaning up after a wedding reception that had been held at the mill, was carrying out the last of the detritus from that celebration when he also became covered in goose bumps. The man checked his watch and noted it was 1:15 p.m. He and Larry Ellis were most interested to note that the accident that had claimed Anna's young life had occurred sometime between one and one-thirty in the afternoon.

What does seem obvious is that although Anna's life was short and tragic, her existence as the spirit of the mill has been enduring and decidedly contented.

One Time Only

Many places remain haunted for years and years. Others are visited only once by a manifestation. The Park House Museum in Amherstburg falls into the latter category. Although there has only been one documented visit from an "other-worldly" being, the encounter had such a profound effect on the one witness that, even though the incident took place nearly a dozen years ago, the woman has steadfastly refused to ever go back into the building.

Sandra Bradt of the City of Windsor Tourist Bureau explained that, considering the house's unorthodox history, it almost deserved to be haunted. The building was constructed in 1796 in Detroit before the international boundaries that we know today had been established. The homeowner had no desire to live under anything but British rule and yet he loved the house that he'd built. This dilemma, he felt, left him no alternative but to dismantle the building, float it downriver and rebuild it in Amherstburg. The plan was certainly a difficult way to establish an address, but at least the man had accomplished his purpose.

The house is now a museum and is, almost all the time, ghost-free. However, long-time staff members vividly remember the day that an apparition joined them. One day in the mid-1980s, a lady visiting the historic site had been touring the inside of the house. The woman spent a considerable amount of time upstairs before coming back down to chat with the museum staff. In the middle of that conversation, the guest excused herself, saying that she wanted to ask a further question of the woman on the second floor with whom she had just been talking.

Park House staff looked at the woman blankly for a moment before recovering sufficient composure to explain that there was no woman upstairs. The guest was adamant and described the woman that she referred to in detail, including that she was wearing a black dress. The museum staff was equally adamant. They knew that there could not possibly be such a woman upstairs in the house. Their discussion had clearly come to an impasse and so the guest made her way up the stairs again to demonstrate her point.

The second floor was as empty as the staff had known it would be, and anyone leaving the house would have had to pass the little group on the ground floor. The poor visitor was badly shaken.

"I guess they had carried on quite a conversation and then the woman just vanished," Sandra Bradt commented.

No one has any idea who the ghost might have been or why she chose that particular day to visit or that particular visitor to interact with, but the day that the apparition put in an appearance is a day that the staff members all still talk about.

Spectres Present Then and Now

Fulford Place in Brockville has been (accurately) called "a tribute to ambition." Indirectly, it is also a tribute to the effectiveness of advertising. George Fulford's beginnings were humble but his dynamism more than made up for the average starting point.

He was born in the mid-1800s. As a young man, he attended a business college, where he apparently acquired a good deal of useful knowledge. At graduation the young man joined his brother in the drugstore business. From there, it didn't take

George long to realize the potential sales possible in the field of patent medicines.

In a fortunate coincidence, a physician named Dr. William Jackson had just developed "Dr. Williams' Pink Pills for Pale People." Fulford took over the manufacturing of this "wonder drug" and advertised it heavily with the promise that "These Pills Make Weak People Strong." Although the inventor never saw much profit from his medical creation, George Fulford made a fortune.

Beginning construction of Fulford Place in 1899 was one of his ways of celebrating that fortune. In order acquire the land to build his planned showplace along the St. Lawrence River, George Fulford bought another mansion—the Edgar Place—and demolished it. Fulford was on his way to acceptance into the area's high society. In 1900, as a "thank you" for his generous support to the Liberal Party, George Fulford became Senator Fulford. His acceptance into the social circles he coveted was now complete.

Fulford Place came alive through entertaining. The family hosted some of the world's most influential people—including heads of state and royalty. But George Fulford was not able to enjoy the fruits of his success for very long. In 1905 he was killed in an accident, leaving three children and his widow, Mary.

Eventually, Fulford Place once again received guests. William Lyon Mackenzie King, at first while Leader of the Opposition, was very fond of travelling to Brockville to visit the late Senator Fulford's widow at her home. Not only did Mary Fulford apparently remind King of his beloved mother, but she also shared his intense interest in communicating with the spirits of the dead. It was here, at Fulford Place, during a three-day visit in February 1932, that King attended his first seance.

Mrs. Fulford invited internationally known medium Henrietta Wriedt, who had conducted seances at Fulford Place for the previous twenty years, to conduct these four seances that included King. All remaining records seem to indicate that Mrs. Wriedt was a legitimately sensitive psychic and not one of the many charlatans who were crowding the field at that time. It seems that despite Wriedt's known difficult financial circumstances, she never charged a great deal of money for her psychic services and remained poor all her life. Many charlatans who were not so gifted, except in the art of deception, used the spiritualism fad of the day as a get-rich-quick scheme.

Specific details of the seances conducted during the three-day visit have been lost to history, but evidently enough entities were brought into Fulford House to satisfy Mrs. Fulford and to entice Canada's future prime minister to become a devotee of such supernatural encounters—for the balance of his life.

Mary Fulford, who died during a thunderstorm, still haunts her beloved home, now a museum operated by the Ontario Heritage Foundation, during storms. The former prime minister, who also died during a severe and eerily localized storm, is said to haunt his former homes, both now museums. (See "Prime Minister Brought Spirit to Ottawa," p. 152.)

Phantom Beasts

The tremendous hormonal surges that youngsters go through during puberty has been known to make some teenagers extremely receptive to paranormal activity happening around them, which they otherwise might not have noticed. It is fitting then, that this age group also has an unusually high incidence of interest in the field. Generally speaking, young people love to read and tell ghost stories, to see horror films and to go to "spooky" places. Of course, part of the reason for their attraction to such pursuits is simply that their parents likely will not approve of them. Therefore, they enter into many of these ventures independent of, and even in defiance of, parental control.

This mix of both cause and effect can make for a volatile combination, as youngsters who go looking for trouble usually find it. This fact was certainly the case in the 1980s with Robert Hedley of Whitby and his high-school friends.

"When I was in high school we used to party in the woods north of Ajax, in an area known as 'Salem's Lot,'" Robert began, before pointing out the connection between the name given to the site and the title of one of Stephen King's spooky novels.

"There were many stories associated with the place," he continued. Predictably, these stories either fell into the "grisly" category or the "scary" category—or both. Equally predictably, not all of the teenagers believed all of the tales— Robert included—until his experience in the early 1990s.

"I had been telling a friend of mine [named] Jay about these stories I had heard in high school. [W]e drove up to the place where the old road used to take us into the spot. Within the five or six years since I had last been there that road had disappeared," Robert recounted.

Only slightly unnerved, the pair decided to continue their explorations.

"We parked the car and proceeded to walk through the woods. We found a path that led [between] two trees with arcane symbols painted on them. We followed the path through the trees and kept walking," he recalled. As they came to an area adjacent to a farmer's field, the two young men decided they were not above a little black humour of their own. They began to carve "a symbol of the Necronomicon [a name coined by occult author H.P. Lovecraft] into the ground" and chuckled as they thought of their mischief frightening future generations of daredevil youngsters. Little did they suspect that their carvings would soon make them the terrified brunt of a supernatural ploy.

Jay and Robert hadn't dug too far into the soil when they discovered that it was concealing a bed of asphalt. By now, they were completely captivated. They decided to dig down below the paving material in the hope of revealing whatever it might be hiding.

The work went slowly and was accompanied by the persistent barking of what sounded like a large dog. Robert later explained that at first it seemed as though the obviously angry animal was roughly "a mile" away, somewhere in the farmer's field. As they continued to dig beneath the asphalt, however, the sounds became louder and more frightening, yet no trace of any animal could be seen.

"Within about fifteen seconds the [barking] sound grew from sounding like one dog to a pack of dogs tearing something apart that just refused to die. And it was getting closer. Within another one to fifteen seconds what had sounded like it was a mile away, sounded like it was fifty feet away, coming through the cornfield...howling, screaming and snarling. [When] it was about fifteen feet from us...the noise was deafening. I turned to Jay and he bolted down the path. I followed. It was dark by then [so] we were tripping and falling over branches and undergrowth but we still ran in a complete panic."

These were not young men who scared easily. Robert described his friend Jay as being the smaller of the two men, "at six foot, one inch in height and 180 pounds. Normally we aren't scared of anything but that night we ran like the hounds of hell were after us."

Once the pair was safely out of the woods, into Robert's car and driving away, they realized that the asphalt that they'd been digging had once been the road that the high-school students had taken into the woods, the road that Robert Hedley had been looking for when he returned with his friend Jay. "I have no idea who [went to such] great effort to ensure [that] it wouldn't be driven down again," Hedley commented. Had the person responsible for burying the road known that there were also vicious-sounding animal spirits protecting whatever was being hidden, then perhaps he might have saved himself some work.

Robert Hedley closed his story with a cryptic comment that this story was only one of many ghost stories from Salem's Lot north of Ajax.

Pirates and buried or sunken treasure are not usually the first images that come to mind when reflecting on Ontario history, but they were all a very real part of our past. Like all legitimate legends, the nuggets of truth in these stories are as intriguingly buried as the treasures they speak of. The legendary origins, however, can usually be attested to by sources as mundane as the shipping records that indicate where ships have sunk, what they were carrying and whether or not they've been salvaged. That there are undiscovered treasures at the bottom of all of the Great Lakes is not a point for debate—it is a fact. Whether or not other treasure lodes exist is less certain.

For instance, not far from Johnstown, beneath the waters of the St. Lawrence Seaway, there may be a stash of thousands of gold coins. There is also a tale that the depths of Opinicon Lake might still hold the silver payroll owed to some of our hard-working pioneers. The story goes that the ship carrying the money to the workers was ambushed by pirates. Seeing that a raid was imminent, the captain noted current compass coordinates and then dumped the kegs of coins overboard.

Not all hidden treasure is submerged. The barrel of gold supposedly buried on a beach has never been found, nor has the chest of gold on Main Duck Island. Both caches have remained an elusive mystery for nearly 250 years.

At least some of Ontario's buried treasure will remain hidden into eternity because it is protected by ghostly guardians. Legend has it that somewhere east of Brockville a group of would-be treasure hunters consulted a psychic before setting out on their trek. The sensitive advised them of a likely area in which to dig. In true legendary fashion, the gentlemen, with visions of gold dancing in their heads, began digging at the witching hour. They hadn't been at their task long when one of the men's shovels struck something solid-sounding. Perhaps he'd hit upon the buried treasure.

Neither they nor we will ever know, however, because just at that instant a team of phantom oxen driven by a grisly looking ghost appeared before the treasure scavengers. The gold seekers scattered into the woods, never to return. If the apparition intended to protect the booty, then it did its job well—to date the hoard has never been uncovered.

Not surprisingly, the men involved that frightening night had more on their minds than accurate identification of the ghostly figures that threatened them, which is probably why there is at least one other version of that tale. The second rendering has manifestations of pigs instead of oxen appearing at the freshly dug pit. The bottom line, however, is the same in both stories. The men, understandably, fled in terror, never to return.

The ghost story surrounding the long-hidden LaRue fortune is considerably better documented, although it predates the tales told above.

In the earliest days of the 1800s when Bella (or Billa, or William) LaRue first feasted his eyes upon the pristine landscape of the St. Lawrence River, its shores and islands, he must have thought that he'd discovered the Garden of Eden. Not content to simply live within the exquisite natural beauty of the area, LaRue also exploited its seemingly endless resources of timber and became a very wealthy man.

Perhaps railing against the truism that "you can't take it with you," the sawmill owner hid a great deal of his money on his land. Attempts to find the buried treasure began as LaRue lay on his deathbed when his favourite daughter, Sarah, asked her ailing father for directions to his cache. He was so ill by then that he wasn't able to speak. He merely pointed toward the window of the room in which he lay. The effort was apparently too much for LaRue: his arm fell back to his side, and he closed his eyes and breathed his last.

Sarah concluded, rightly or wrongly, that her father's gesture meant that the hiding place could be seen from the bedroom window. Right away the family began digging—first, the man's grave was dug and then they began to dig numerous holes in the deceased's property to see if they could turn up the riches they were sure were hidden somewhere nearby.

Word of the frustrating treasure hunt spread throughout the community. Locals came onto the LaRue land armed with divining rods, spades and shovels. The experience of one such group was so dramatic that it has been preserved in the annals of the area's local history as a first-person narrative.

One day, long after sunset, four treasure hunters slipped quietly onto the LaRue estate. Presumably the cover of night served the purpose of making the men more difficult to see, in the first place to hide the fact that they were trespassing on private property and then, if their mission was successful, to defray unwanted attention as they carted away the spoils. Only the unobstructed glow of moonlight illuminated the men's undertaking.

Armed with a witch-hazel divining rod, they began walking the area popularly thought to conceal the riches. When the branch gave a quiver and pointed to the ground, the men were overjoyed. They were sure that all that stood between them and great wealth was a little digging. As they began shovelling earth away from the spot that they were sure held the treasure, the devious little group was boisterous and confident.

Soon, however, their energy began to wane and, by coincidence, with it went their illumination. Clouds had scuttled across the sky, blocking out the light of the moon. Moments later, the wind picked up and howled through the trees in the nearby forest. Trying to ignore the rapidly changing conditions, the four kept at their task. Suddenly a sharp, chill blast of cold air rushed among them, shocking their bodies which were overheated from exertion.

Just as they were reacting to the sudden, unnatural wind, one man's shovel suddenly hit upon something solid. A clanging sound rang out in the night—the sound of the metal shovel blade hitting something metal in the ground. They ignored the eerily changing weather that had suddenly surrounded them and knelt beside the pit they had dug. Frantically clawing at the earth with their hands, the men were finally rewarded. There, within their grasp, lay something smooth and flat, something manufactured, something that had been purposely buried.

Using their shovels now as levers, the men began to try to pry open what they supposed was a lid of the coveted treasure chest. And that's when they heard "it." As one of the men who was there reported, "it" was the sound of distant hooves "trampling upon the earth in the distance, as if the guardian spirit of the treasure trove was marshalling all his cohorts to hurl back the audacious invaders who had thus dared to desecrate his domains and snatch away the glittering coins confided to his care."

Panic seized the men. They looked around and saw that they were surrounded by apparitions of black cattle. Judging by the thundering sounds that the hooves are reported to have made, there must have been thousands of the phantom beasts.

The men dropped their tools and fled from the spot as quickly as they were able. They kept running as long as they could but once they reached the house that had once belonged to the man whose treasure they were seeking to steal, they stopped and caught their collective breaths. Once their panic abated and their breathing returned to normal patterns, they noticed something very strange. The sky was as clear now as it had been when they'd begun their ill-fated adventure. The sky was cloudless, the wind still and the land moonlit.

Feeling somewhat foolish at their panic-stricken flight, the men decided to return to the excavation. After all, they had actually seen the chest that held the treasure. All that was left to do now was to open it up and remove the coins. To a man, they were very soon going to be wealthy beyond their wildest dreams. Such a reward was well worth overcoming a bit of self-conscious fear.

The pit was much as they left it—their coats and shovels on the ground surrounding it. The phantom beasts had disappeared, apparently taking the treasure chest they were guarding along with them.

Further Reading

Boyer, Dwight. 1968. *Ghost Ships of the Great Lakes*. New York: Dodd Mead and Co.

Grange Newsletter, The. April 1995. Toronto.

Hoy, Claire. 1985. *Bill Davis*. Toronto: Metheun Press.

Gervais, C.H. and James Reaney. 1976. *Baldoon*. Erin: Porcupine's Quill.

Lamb, Marjorie and Barry Pearson. 1976. *The Boyd Gang*. Toronto: Peter Martin and Associates.

Lambert, R.S. 1955. *Exploring the Supernatural*. Toronto: McClelland & Stewart.

Little, William T. 1970. *The Tom Thomson Mystery*. Toronto: McGraw-Hill.

MacLean, Harrison John. 1974. *The Fate of the Griffon*. Toronto: Griffin Press Limited.

McClement, Fred. 1974. *The Strange Case of Ambrose Small*. Toronto: McClelland & Stewart.

McDonald, Neil T., updated by Alan Mann. 1986. *The Baldoon Mystery*. Wallaceburg: Standard Press.

McFarlane, Brian. 1995. *The Leafs*. Toronto: Stoddart Publishing.

Melady, John. 1988. *Overtime, Overdue: The Bill Barilko Story*. Trenton: City Print.

Owen, Iris M., with Margaret Sparrow. 1976. *Conjuring up Philip, An Adventure in Psychokinesis*. Toronto: Fitzhenry & Whiteside.

Reaney, James. 1983. *The Donnellys, a Trilogy*. Victoria: Press Porcepic.

Salts, J. Robert. 1996. *You Are Never Alone; Our Life on the Donnelly Homestead*. London: Self-published.

Smith, Barbara. 1993. *Ghost Stories of Alberta*. Toronto: Hounslow Press.

Smith, Barbara. 1997. *Ghost Stories of Manitoba*. Edmonton: Lone Pine Publishing.

Smith, Barbara. 1996. *More Ghost Stories of Alberta*. Edmonton: Lone Pine Publishing.

Smith, Barbara. 1997. *Passion & Scandal, Great Canadian Love Stories*. Calgary: Detselig Enterprises.

Wallace, W. Stewart. 1931. *Murders and Mysteries, A Canadian Series*. Connecticut: Hyperion Press Incorporated.